Edith Templeton was born in Prague in 1916. Both sides of her family were big estate owners in Bohemia. (Her father, who was a doctor of technology, received, when leaving school, a gold medal from the Emperor Franz Joseph for being the best finalist in the whole Austro-Hungarian Empire.) Edith was educated at the French Lycée and then at the Prague Medical University for three years and, after several short stays in England, she settled, at the age of twenty-two, first in Cheltenham and then in London. She married Dr Edmund Ronald, for twenty years a brilliant cardiologist in India, physician to the King of Nepal, first European to enter its royal palace, and *éminence grise* in that country. While with him in Calcutta, she met Nehru, the Dalai Lama and the Panchen Lama and, of course, quite a few maharajahs. She has since lived, apart from her first four years in Vienna and afterwards her native city, in Salzburg, Lausanne, Torremolinos, Estoril and Italy. During the war she worked for the American War Office, in the office of the Surgeon General, and from 1945-6 was a captain with the British Forces in Germany as Conference and Law Court interpreter.

Although she started writing at the age of four – her first story being published when she was ten – Edith Templeton's first novel, *Summer in the Country*, was not published until 1950. Its success was followed by *Living on Yesterday* (1951) and *The Island of Desire* (1952) – all three are being published by The Hogarth Press. She is also the author of several other volumes of fiction, as well as many short stories and magazine articles, having been a regular contributor to the likes of *Vogue, Harpers* and the *New Yorker*. She has one son and now lives in Bordighera, on the Italian Riviera.

SUMMER IN THE COUNTRY

Edith Templeton

New Introduction by
Anita Brookner

THE HOGARTH PRESS
LONDON

Published in 1985 by
The Hogarth Press
40 William IV Street, London WC2N 4DF

First published in Great Britain by Eyre and Spottiswoode Ltd 1950
Hogarth edition offset from the original British edition
Copyright Etta Trust Reg., Vaduz
Introduction copyright © Anita Brookner 1985

British Library Cataloguing in Publication Data

Templeton, Edith
Summer in the country.
I. Title
823'.914[F]   PR6070.E4
ISBN 0 7012 0575 X

Printed in Great Britain by
Cox & Wyman Ltd
Reading, Berkshire

INTRODUCTION

The writer of fiction is a stateless person, or perhaps should be, for that condition would automatically exclude those radically inauthentic compositions built around a formula ('. . . three generations of women . . . from the peat-bogs of Killarney to the pent-houses of Manhattan . . .') which seem to flourish these days and are read, by the credulous and the not so credulous, as an aid to modern living. Edith Templeton's novels are also an aid to living, but of a different kind. For the state of exile in which she writes represents both her inner and her outer world; she has lived in many countries since she left her native Prague at the age of nineteen, and although equally at home, or not at home, in Paris, in Torremolinos, in Estoril, in Salzburg, in Katmandu, or, today, in Bordighera, she is at all times definitively removed from her birthplace and from the way of life to which she so constantly refers: the life of the country gentry of central Europe in the years immediately preceding World War Two.

When Edith Templeton's first novel, *Summer in the Country*, was published in 1950, more than one critic compared her with Maupassant and Turgenev. This showed creditable expertise, but perhaps a more mature eye would discard Maupassant and retain Turgenev; certainly she would have it so. Melancholy, irony, elegance: these qualities underline the comparison, but Edith Templeton's novels, which are not so slight as they appear at first reading (a characteristic they share with those of Turgenev) have, in addition to these qualities, a worldliness all the more supreme for being understated, as worldliness always should be. Like Jean Rhys, whom she greatly admires, she is one of those singular *déracinées* whose fictional tone of voice occasionally has the edge over the native product, and which, in certain important matters, can be relied upon to be less sentimental, less tactless, and less self-conscious than their English counterpart.

Edith Templeton would also claim as her literary mentor Theodor Fontane, whose novel *Effi Briest* so effortlessly conveys the sense not only of a broken heart but of a broken reputation, both equally important, for in this world behaviour is vital: behaviour remains one's stamp more than wealth, more than circumstance, perhaps even more than birth. He has no heart, says a character in her finest novel, *Living on Yesterday*. 'No heart. And no manners. And I don't know which is worse.' Both, of course, are inexcusable, and there is a sense in all Edith Templeton's novels that the villain of the piece will be recognized by his lack of good manners, while the peripateia of the plot will finally show him to be lacking in heart. Yet although these novels are essentially novels of manners, they are also something more, for running beneath the social comedy, so beautifully conducted by all the principal players, there lie acts of madness, of revenge, and of revolt, resorted to in extreme moments, but – and this is the singular thing – never regretted. It is the strange completeness of these acts, and the density of the context in which they are committed, that give Edith Templeton's novels their unusual savour.

Turgenev, Jean Rhys, Fontane: I would add Schnitzler, for that dash of Viennese concentration on intrigue. All these strains add up to a world of great complexity and apparent simplicity, a world in which everything is foreign and everything has enormous style. Here is a gentleman's study, from *Living on Yesterday:*

Although the library faced south and had three windows, it was a sombre room. The moss-green velvet hangings were never completely drawn aside, and the ruched and gathered tulle curtains, once white, were now so dusty that each fold was traced with a line of grey. The divan was draped with a Persian rug and strewn with cushions of gold and silver brocade, the covers of which could easily have been identified by old friends of the family as being discarded ball dresses of the late lamented Mrs Marek. The black bookcases reached to the ceiling and were filled in such a manner that the finely bound and gilt edged volumes stood on the upper and middle shelves, while the paper-backed and bedraggled books occupied the lower regions, irrespective of their contents. A settee and two armchairs of red repp were grouped in a corner near the stove round a table with a blue and red brocade cover trimmed with a tarnished gold fringe, and all the other stands and shelves and small tables in the room had similar brocade covers. Even the small and fashionable objects which litter a man's room, the case for playing cards and the brush for the card table, the appointments book and the blotter, were backed with brocade and enriched with gold braid. A lamp with a domed brown shade was suspended by brass chains from the ceiling like a sinister mushroom.

And here is a meal:

There had been iced clear meat soup with pastry triangles filled with liver, followed by potato pancakes with a ragout of mushrooms, after which came roast veal speckled by strips of pickled cucumber and bacon and surrounded by bone-marrow dumplings and cream gravy and accompanied by a green salad with a crown of hard-boiled eggs. At present they were eating curly squares of fried batter with a wine sauce, which in this part of Bohemia is called 'God's mercies'.

Clearly, nothing could be more removed from the country-house living of the English shires: from these sumptuously fed and curiously decorated people one is entitled to expect singularity, sophistication, and almost certainly brutality. Like the characters in Tchekhov's *Cherry Orchard*, they are going to get their own way and keep it. Their estates may be broken up and sold, they may be dispossessed, they may stand to lose everything, but they will nevertheless have the last word.

The plot of *Summer in the Country* is in fact very like that of *The Cherry Orchard*. The castle of Kirna, near Brandys in central Bohemia, is maintained lazily, expensively, and at a loss. It houses old Mrs Birk, and her brother Tony, Mrs Birk's daughters, Alice and Bettine, and many servants. The young lawyer who visits the family is nervously aware that he is an outsider and indeed that there is no way in which he might become an insider, for all the talk at table is of family matters, the jokes are family jokes, the allusions are family allusions. It is in fact one of those maddening families which continually and relentlessly reclaims its own and for whom the outside world and its inhabitants have only a peripheral existence. The young lawyer has been brought in as a prospect for the second daughter, Bettine, but of course he is not quite up to the mark; his function in the novel is to indicate the marginality of anyone who is not born into the clan. However, even more marginal is Oscar Ritter, the boorish millionaire who has married Mrs Birk's granddaughter and Alice's daughter, Margot. It is Oscar's money which is keeping them all going, but they pay dearly for the favour, particularly Margot, whose defiance and irritation can be sensed not through anything outrageous in her own speech but through the whining self-importance and importunity of Oscar, who sets the reader's nerves on edge quite as much as those of the members of the family. In any event, Oscar is no gentleman; he wears his bedroom slippers outside the bedroom, which my own grand-mother said should never be done, in any circumstances.

The denouement of this tale cannot be foreseen by the reader and is all the more shocking for that. Yet the even tenor of life at Kirna nevertheless effortlessly survives, and good manners prevail to the very end. However, a sadness remains, and it is the sadness of the knowledge that once certain acts have been committed *nothing* can be retrieved. It is a moral sadness, and for the attentive reader it is there throughout the book. It is also a very funny book. Mrs Birk dislikes her daughter, the insufferable Alice, but of course would never permit herself to think so; she is much too polite for that. But her opinions escape her from time to time, although the manner of their utterance is so imperturbable that the nervous lawyer, Marek, is even more put out. 'Would you like some of this sherry, Mr Marek? There is whiskey and gin, if you prefer it, but you'll have to wait till my daughter Alice comes. She keeps it locked up. It gives her something to do'.

These people are enormously experienced. They are ex-perienced in a way which is not common in England, and their author, who was in her early thirties when she wrote this, her first novel, was born into this kind of experience. It is almost unnerving to realize that English is not her native tongue, for only a few tiny traces of hesitation show here and there, and they are balanced by the kind of perfect paragraph that has one holding one's breath to the last full stop: 'The old lady looked into the distance with unseeing eyes. "I went to school with him. He sat at my table." How often had she heard these protests, childish and desperate, which people utter when they have been betrayed; as though the blow could have come from anybody else except their friends.'

I have said that the author was in her early thirties when she wrote this, her first book. But in fact she had begun to write long before that. She started when she was four years old and had her first story printed, at the age of ten, in the Sunday edition of the *Prager Tagblatt*. Like all true writers, she does not know where the plots or the words come from, and she certainly never knows when they are about to come. The good news, from Bordighera, is that there may be more on the way. For new readers, of whom there will be many, *Summer in the Country* is an introduction to a distinctive and unusual literary talent.

Anita Brookner, Bordighera – London 1984

PHILINTE

Serait-il à propos et de la bienséance
De dire à mille gens tout ce que d'eux on pense?
Et quand on a quelqu'un qu'on haït ou qui déplaît,
Lui doit-on déclarer la chose comme elle est?

Le Misanthrope,
Acte 1, Scène 1
MOLIÈRE

CHAPTER 1

A VISITOR was expected in the afternoon at Castle Kirna. The stable clock above the baroque frieze of horses struck two while a boy was harnessing a pair of chestnut cobs to a landau amidst a flutter of pigeons and sparrows. From the far end of the yard, by the gate flanked with stone poodles, the old coachman stood and watched. His plaited whip was tucked so carelessly under his arm that the scarlet tassel trailed over the cobblestones.

Inside the castle several clocks were still chiming the hour when Mr. Birk trampled into his sister's drawing-room.

'I'm getting the horses ready for the three-five train, Ida,' he said.

'Yes. I thought it would be about time,' answered the old lady and glanced at him sideways before turning her attention to the game of patience on the satinwood table in front of her.

He stepped up nearer and began to rub his hands up and down his breeches, lost in thought.

'I think I'll drive myself. Yes. That's it.' He slapped his thigh noisily. 'That settles it. I'll fetch him from the station myself, that creature of yours, that visitor, and I'll tell Prochazka he can trot off home now. He's got out the open landau and the cob mares. They'll do for your chap, I suppose. What do you say?'

'They'll do, Tony.' She paused, her hand hovering above a card, taking it up, putting it down again. 'Why are you sending Prochazka away?'

He walked to the window, rubbing his worn breeches.

'Because he's had a bad night of it, sitting up with Melody and giving her cold compresses. And you can tell your madam daughter that next time she feeds that horse again with fresh grass, I'll drag her out of bed and down to the stables, and she can sit up with her and nurse her through the colic. When you get to Prochazka's age you don't feel like frolicking about after a night like this; you can tell that to your daughter. Why, he must be – let me see – the parents were still alive when he took over – well anyway, he must be getting on to seventy.'

'Tony,' said the old lady, 'when you get to Zelenec, ask the stationmaster if the pineapples have arrived yet.'

'Pineapples – what do you want pineapples for?'

'To be eaten as dessert, Tony.'

'Don't tell me. I'm not a fool. Of course they'll be eaten. Hang it all, what I meant was, what's the good of it? Did we get any pineapples when we were young, I ask you? And what next? First pineapples and then I suppose it will be electricity. That damned agent of yours has been button-holing me again today.'

'You engaged him, Tony.'

'I did. So I did. What do you expect me to do about it?

Bend my knees and ask for pardon? Of course I engaged him. I'm not snivelling about it. I always stand up to my actions. I couldn't know that the fellow was bitten by the development bug, could I? I think he's got an electric gadget where other people have a heart. Still, I'll tell you that much, Ida. When it comes to horses, I can stand up to any Irishman or Hungarian – the wretched traitors – and it has taken me a lifetime to get to know a horse when I see one. Well, you can't be a judge of men on top of it, can you? Life's too short for that.'

'That's true, Tony.' She scrutinized the cards. 'Still,' she continued, 'the agent is right, I think. We've got the mill-stream and the mill has not been used for years now and probably never will be worked again. All that waterpower could be put to good use.'

He turned abruptly and trampled to the door. 'Well, I'm not interested in the good use; I won't waste the money on it, so long as I hold my share of Kirna. When I'm dead you can do what you want. That agent can't leave anything alone. It breaks his heart if something does not serve a purpose. He'd – find a useful job for the flies, if he could. I'm off now. And don't worry, I'll see to your pine-apples.'

Before she had time to reply, he was out of the room with the swiftness of movement that is often surprisingly found in heavy-built people.

Mr. Birk crossed the hall hurriedly and with quick bends of his head, born from a lifetime's habit, he avoided the antlers and stuffed animals' heads that bristled on every wall above the wainscoting of imitation leather, tooled and gilded in the Spanish style. A few moments later he stood in the yard, holding court among the coachman, the groom and a stable-boy. Above his head a number of pigeons clustered round the turret and the clock.

'That's understood then, Prochazka, off you go,' he said and touched the old man's lapel.

'That's understood, sir,' came the answer. 'Now, let me see. You'll be wanting the whip. No, this one's not good enough for you; it's all sweaty where you grip it.' He suddenly turned to the stable-boy and yelled at him as though the youth were on a parade ground and not standing close by: 'Run and get the new whip for the master, above the bridle hooks in the harness room.' He then resumed his respectful voice and attitude, while the groom, without saying a word, picked up a stone and aimed it with precision at the running boy's behind.

'Gee up, that will warm thee!' guffawed Mr. Birk, and walked towards the carriage.

Like most men of his class and generation, he affected that crude and cheerfully inarticulate jargon of the stable and the hunting-field which is spoken in the regimental cavalry messes and among the big estate-owners in all parts of the world, and according to which there is not a situation in life which cannot be expressed in the terms of the horse and hound.

While his master mounted the box with great lightness, Prochazka stood by and gave a smart salute. His gesture held a flourish, his moustache was jauntily twirled, the silver buttons on his old livery gleamed. He had been dashing once and was not willing to forget it. As the landau rolled away, he remained still for a while and listened to the crack of the whip, the clatter of the hooves, the rumble of the wheels and the screech of startled hens until their echo had died away from the cobblestones.

CHAPTER 2

I T W A S a dreamy journey across the ripe and hot countryside. The dust lay white and velvety on the highway, turned the grassy ditches grey and silvered the small blue plums that grow alongside the roads in this part of Bohemia.

There was not a soul in sight. A few cottages were passed, thatched and whitewashed, with lace curtains and fuchsia pots behind the windows, with a green latticed fence enclosing the garden filled with hollyhocks, sunflowers and love-lies-bleeding and guarded by a drowsy watchdog.

Mr. Birk arrived at the station in good time. A group of children assembled around him from nowhere and he entrusted the horses to them. Then he passed beyond the barriers and approached a railwayman and dismissed his salute with a wave of his hand.

'Look here, Zavadil,' he said. 'I'm going along to the stationmaster's to see after a blasted case of pineapples. Now, when the three-five comes in and you collect the tickets, watch out for a man for me, will you? Another guest for the old lady. And tell him to wait and hang about with him till I come back. Don't know what he looks like, but you are as good at picking them out as I am. They are all the same. Seedy and weedy and coffee-housing written all over them. You know the types as well as I do. Cheerio.' And he took two cigarettes out of his case and handed them to the man.

The visitor, on alighting on the platform, had been searching in vain for a motor-car – an old-fashioned limousine perhaps, or an open touring car, and was taken aback when he was conducted to a broad and clumsy-looking carriage, painted yellow and covered inside with black waxcloth, drawn by two overfed and clumsy-looking horses. He stood and stared at the gaping children, the dogs continually lifting a leg against the wheels, and the swarm of flies. He had not expected this.

The Birks kept open house in Prague and entertained in a big style without being ostentatious. Good living was taken so much for granted by them that it had lost the appearance of luxury. Like all the people who came in touch with them, he knew that they lived for a part of the year on their estate in the country which was the source from which their income flowed – a manor house or country seat of sorts. In the past, when thinking of the receptions he had attended, of the aristocratic old woman who moved through the suite of drawing-rooms from one group of guests to another against a background of brown damask and red velvet, extending a beautiful white hand – the more convinced he had become that a castle was her natural home. He thought of her in the theatre, seated in the box which the family rented every season, dressed in black lace and diamonds, surrounded by her two daughters, her grandchild and a friend or two, surveying the scene from beneath discreetly lowered eyelids or consulting the programme through a raised golden lorgnon. He recalled the few occasions when he had been asked to one of their small musical gatherings and had been impressed by the manner in which his hostess had talked of the various topics of the day, of art and politics, with great ease and authority and without ever using the fashionable small-talk of society. All this he had borne in mind when he had received his invitation to Kirna and been told: 'We live very simply there; I hope you will not expect too much.' He had smiled with polite incredulity and had gratefully accepted.

'Aha, aha, glad to see you, young man; in she goes, Zavadil; good man, now put the suitcase on top. Prop it against the seat, Zavadil; that's it. The young gentleman will sit with me on the box. Now, what is heavier, Zavadil, a pound of pineapples or a pound of lead? Haha, he knows it, he knows the answer, the old fox. Now be off, you brats, you lords and ladies, you little bits of filth. Give my compliments to mother and ask her if she can solve the riddle.' Mr. Birk guffawed and slapped his thigh. 'There you are, that's got rid of them.'

'It was very good of you to fetch me,' said the visitor and after a second added 'Sir'. He decided it would be better to be on the safe side. The old boy talked the dialect of the country folk, but that was common use among the landed gentry, and he had the authoritative air of an ex-officer. He had been right.

'I am Birk, Tony Birk, at your service, sir. My sister commanded me to fetch you. And you are – now, don't tell me – don't tell me – you must be one of the Mareks – wait a minute – I know the face. Either the leather Mareks or the silk Mareks. Now, which?'

'Leather, sir.'

'There you are. Old Polda is your father then. Right? And are you the eldest?'

'No, the second, Mr. Birk.'

'Never mind. Can't always be the first. And what do you do for a living, young Marek?'

'I am a lawyer, Mr. Birk.'

'Aha. The brains of the family. I'll have to be on my guard with you. Now, let's be off. That's all you've got, this one suitcase, is it? Fine. Now, on the box with you. Step on the front wheel. I'll give you a leg up. Shame on you, a young whipper-snapper like you! Try again. And mind that nice grey suit of yours. I bet that's from Frey's. Hem. Thought so. I wish I could afford him.'

'I wish you could,' thought Marek as he wedged himself into his seat. He did not know that the cost of the old man's riding-boots alone could have paid for three suits of the famous tailor.

'Have a cigarette, Marek. What's your Christian name ?'

'Raoul.'

'Have a cigarette, Raoul. And call me Tony.' He held out his case. 'We don't stand on ceremony here. We are poor and simple people.'

'By God, I'll say you are poor,' thought Raoul as he helped himself from the battered pinchbeck etui. He did not know that the horses' harness was of solid silver, enough to provide the whole Marek family with silver cigarette-cases and to spare.

'It is not much of a country to look at,' said Mr. Birk, while they jogged along in a comfortable trot, and he cracked his whip from time to time, careful not to touch the horses.

'I suppose not,' said Raoul, looking about him. There were fields on end as far as he could see, sparsely honeycombed by roads and lanes, all of them bordered with ditches and lined with plum trees. At the rim of the horizon stretched a deep blue band of forest, and a church spire was visible beyond it.

'A bit flat,' he ventured.

'As flat as flat,' affirmed Mr. Birk cheerfully. 'As flat as the bosom of my cousin Masa, haha. Not that she can help it, bless her soul. No, this isn't Switzerland, my boy. But what the land hasn't got outside, it's got inside it all right. One of the best stretches of beet-growing soil in Europe, my boy, make no mistake about it. All ours, as far as you can see and further! When you came from Prague, from the second but last station before you got here, the land belongs to the family. Not bad, eh?'

'Very nice,' murmured the other. 'What is the church over there? Does that belong to the village?'

'Lord no. The village has no church. That's the church in Brandys you are seeing. That's a town, a proper little town.'

'Oh yes?'

'It used to be a garrison in the old days. The Dragoons were stationed there, the regiment of the Archduke Charles who became Emperor afterwards in nineteen-sixteen. Not that he lasted long. But I still say, if he had had the sense to march into Prague in eighteen and have himself crowned King of Bohemia, the whole mess could have been prevented.

Even the Hungarians, the wretched traitors, would have come to heel. Still, that's not what I was going to say, we'll have a talk about that another day. Yes. Brandys. There were some goings on in those days, let me tell you! I was stationed there, too, in my time; under another Archduke, though – it's longer ago than you can remember. I was forty years prettier then, haha! Many's the time we used to throw the grand piano out of the window of the Mess. And my old father would pay up every time on the nail. Without blinking an eyelash. In those days, if you did not have a crown embroidered above your initials, my boy, you had to cough up pretty heavily. It isn't everybody that has served with the Dragoons. Of course, that was still under the old Emperor. When the Archduke Charles took over, it was not the same thing any more. I'll drive you over to Brandys one day and I'll show you the corner where the onion woman had her stand. A horrible old harridan she was, selling onions, you know the way they do it, all strung up on raffia and tied into a sort of wreath. Well, every time the Archduke passed her, he would stop and buy a wreath of onions and hang them round his neck, believe it or not, and prance like this through the town.'

He cocked his head to one side like an old dog who listens to a far away and reminiscent sound. For a while they rolled on without speaking. A white terrier shot out from one of the cottage gardens and the horses reared and swerved dangerously near the ditch.

'That was Vancura's dog,' said Mr. Birk and chuckled. 'It just shows you, you must never slacken the reins. Now, if Prochazka had been driving, you would have picked your bones out from the ditch, take my word for it. He always goes fast asleep on the box as soon as he gets going. Now we'll cut through the bridle path on the left here and see if we catch them in Semtin. Not supposed to go that way with a car. Still, never mind.'

'Is that another village?'

'No fear. It's where my brother Max hangs out. I don't think you have met him; he hardly ever comes to Prague these days. He's got a cottage over there; we'll come to it in a minute. Just a small place and a garden, but he is rolling in money, make no mistake about it. He works like a dog. He could buy us out any day he wanted to.'

After a few minutes of what seemed very insecure driving, the path widened and they approached a large yard, humming with the sound of a thrashing-machine and peopled by numerous farmworkers who looked very small against the vast masses of iron and the giant stacks of grain. Behind it lay a low manor house with the yellow walls and the green shutters that had been so usual in the Austrian Imperial days. Raoul felt dazed by the clamour around him and the sight of the steadily turning ribbon which carried the grain in a never-ending stream to the machine. It was to him like a sunlit nightmare.

'Aha, here they are,' roared Mr. Birk. From the other side of the path, from a copse of hazel bushes, elders and dog roses, emerged a St. Bernard with clumsy undulating movements. After him arrived two Alsatians tied to each other by a strip of leather and making awkward progress. Behind them three young men in white.

A moment later the carriage was surrounded by them,

and while Raoul tried stealthily to wipe his hands wetted by the slobbering St. Bernard, he was introduced by his companion, who was shouting and slapping his thigh, obviously regarding it all as a huge joke, although Raoul could not see why it should be so funny to meet relatives whom the old man was probably in the habit of meeting frequently.

'These are the young Maxes, you see; not all of them, mind you, because he's got six brats – only three just to begin with, haha. Come here, you rascals, and meet another rascal from Prague, Raoul Marek. That's young Max, the one who looks half baked, and that's Jenda and that's Lolo – they are a bit daft, too, if you ask me.'

They were all of medium height and good-looking in an impudent way. Their wide cheekbones, their rather low foreheads under the sleek blond hair, and the tip-tilted noses spoke of generations of peasant stock, but the narrow feet, the fine wrists and the shape of the head showed that they were of gentle birth. Attired as they were in white silk shirts and off-white flannels, they could have stood under the arched colonnade of any international Spa. But glancing downwards Raoul saw that the turn-overs of their trousers were criss-crossed with bits of chaff and grain stalks, and their beautifully made slim shoes were crusted with flakes of dung and caked with mud.

'We are having a skittle alley built at the back of the garden, Uncle Tony. Will you come and look at it?'

'Marketa is in Biarritz and she sends her love.'

'What do you think of the old man's idea, Uncle Tony, the way he rigged up Rollo and Rex? Don't you think it's capital. He got so sick and tired of being dragged about by

19

them on the leash that he tied them up, and now they can worry each other.'

'Do you know that the great Dane bitch is dead? You remember she was in whelp? The old man is furious. She had a litter of eight. They all had crooked legs; it was the dachshund who had done it, haha. Now, what we can't understand – how the deuce did he manage it? He is a deuce of a dog. The old man is livid. Tell Aunt Ida, will you?'

'I'll tell her all right. Now I must be off, boys. Got to deliver my charge.'

'Uncle Tony, do you know, Vaclav says he saw Uncle Karel the other night, as clear as daylight. He was sitting by the table and suddenly Uncle Karel was on the chair opposite him. And then he vanished. Will you tell them at Kirna?'

'The hell I will. Get away with you. Vaclav's been in his cups as always. That's how he saw Karel. Now stand back there. When are you coming over?'

'On Sunday, Uncle Tony. And we kiss Aunt Ida's hand. Will Margot be back on Sunday?'

'I suppose so. She is bringing her dear husband with her. Now hold on to your dirty mongrels, boys, and when you come, mind you don't bring them over or Bettine will have hysterics, you know what she's like, and Alice will have something to say, and we'll never see the end of it. So long, boys.'

'They are good boys, you know,' said Mr. Birk when they had regained the highway. 'But Max lets them run wild. Indulges them too much. The way they run round among the beets in their six-hundred-crown shoes from Budapest – Prague won't do for them, you know – it's wicked. He brings them up as wasters and rotters.'

'What was that about Uncle Karel?' asked Raoul Marek. 'Who is he? Why did he tell it in that manner?'

'Uncle Karel was my sister's husband. He's been dead for the last fifteen years. Died of a disease, you know.'

'Oh, was that Mrs. Birk-Borovec's husband?'

'No. Not Ida's. My other sister's husband. My sister Louise. But how the hell am I to tell her that Vaclav got sozzled and saw a ghost. We don't speak, you know. Not for the last twenty years. And don't you tell Ida about it, either. She doesn't speak to her either. Look here, I'd better tell you. When you come to Kirna, you'll probably see an old woman. Looks like a servant, but worse than a servant, if you know what I mean. Our maids wear black and white aprons. But she wears a black apron, black alpaca. You can't miss it. That's my sister Louise. She sold out her share of Kirna years ago to us. The same time that Max did; that's when he built his hut over there – you've just seen it. Well, we don't talk to her; family matters – you know how it is. But she comes up to the castle year after year and stays there in summer. She is so mean that she will not pay for holidays. So she goes to Kirna. We can't stop her, can we? She has always diddled everybody. She is a rich woman, but she eternally wears her blasted apron, so that she won't wear her dresses out. You wouldn't believe it. And every morning she gets up at five and goes to the orchard and picks up the windfalls so that the gardeners and the farmworkers can't have them. And yet the fruit are all for the asking! Why, we could supply the whole of Brandys and Zelenec with apples. Funny, isn't it?'

'Very,' said Raoul Marek.

'So when you see her, just pass by and don't you take any notice of her. You know how it is.'

'I will, Mr. Birk,' agreed Raoul Marek. And in his mind's eye he visualized a long and ardent family law suit, where an inheritance of millions was involved. He did not know that twenty years ago sister Louise had sued her own daughter for a sewing machine which she had lent her and which her daughter refused to return. That she had asked her sister Ida to appear in court as witness. Her sister had refused, because she felt it to be beneath her dignity to stand up in court and give evidence on behalf of this domestic utensil. That brother Tony had at the same time given her daughter a birthday present, more costly than was his custom, and that Louise had drawn from that the conclusion that he too sided with her daughter and against her and that he and Ida were her mortal enemies. . . .

'Now we are getting to Kirna village – Great Kirna, as it is called correctly, hahaha. Really. I am not joking,' remarked Mr. Birk cheerfully. 'And once we are out on the road again, we'll take the fork to the left and you'll see a long wall. That's where the park begins. Behind that wall. It's as high as a house and we stick glass shards on the top of it, but the devils climb over just the same; you wouldn't believe it.'

'What is there to steal, Mr. Birk? Surely, a park – not very attractive.'

'Oh, just wood, you know – firewood, logs, anything like that. Old Kocour does the rounds every night with a gun and a dog. If you ask me, he sleeps in the agent's office as snugly as anybody else does. Never sees or hears a soul.'

'But surely, Mr. Birk, if you had several dogs running all over the estate——'

'No good at all, Raoul. Sometimes they get up to something big, like when they stole clover seed out of the storing place. In that case they poison all the dogs that are about. I lost two like this during the last three years. One was a beauty of a puppy. I had started to have him walked——' He flicked his whip and spat to the ground. 'It's no good, I tell you.'

They skirted the park wall at an exhilarating speed, as the horses were nearing the stables. Looking back over his shoulder through the cloud of dust, the young man saw the dark mass of trees above the stone wall – they must have been hundreds of years old. He looked ahead again and there they continued, above the wall, as far as he could see. He fastened his eyes on the dancing whip right in front of him, on the tassel plaited of scarlet and honey-coloured leather, but the trees stood behind it with the eloquent silence of unknown living things. He felt uncomfortable.

'We are almost there now,' said Mr. Birk in a comforting tone, as though he had guessed the young man's thoughts. 'Hope you won't be disappointed. Hope you won't feel dull. You won't find much going on, you know. Got a book with you? I don't have to look twice at you to know that it's no good offering you a hunter or a gun. Haha. Why, that face of yours is as smooth as an egg. Haven't seen much of wind and weather. Eh?'

'You are quite right, sir. But I brought a book along. Enough for the few days, I think.'

'Splendid. Now, see that gate with the animals on it? If

you are polite, you'll call them lions. Now, what's that book you've got? *Memoirs of Casanova*, I bet.'

'Not as bad as that, Mr. Birk. Actually – it's psychology – dreams and the unconscious.'

'Aha – might have known it was something brainy.'

The horses turned into an ill-kept gravel drive, damp and shadowy under the foliage curving above their heads. They walked at a pace. A screeching of poultry came muffled from a distance, where the two stone poodles guarded the entrance to the yet invisible castle.

'I know all about this stuff. This psychology. This modern hocus-pocus. Why, I've known it for years, before they ever thought of it. Take a horse, for instance. When you start to jump a horse, you are supposed to canter it to warm it up and then you jump. Now, a beginner, as likely as not, canters it on and then – in the last moment – when he faces the hurdle – the horse stops dead and shoots him over its head. Why? Because subconsciously, as you would call it, the rider is afraid to jump and the horse in its horse's brain knows it and does what the rider really wants – it stops dead. Horses are no fools, you know; they always know what's in your mind. We conceal it more. So you see, Raoul, if I was a horse – I would stop driving on now – and I'd take you straight back to the station.'

The young man went pale. He looked at the old man, at the white bristly head, at the clear eyes, at the red nose and the hanging cheeks, at the patched and frayed linen coat, at the worn breeches, and he opened his mouth and shut it again.

The landau crunched over the drive and the young man braced himself to come face to face with the castle at any moment. He did not know what he imagined it to be like he only knew that it would not be up to much. The horses curved their necks and set the harness jingling as they cantered over the cobblestones of the yard. He lost his breath as he was thrown forward and back again, and was still gasping when they halted. He looked dismayed on the huge farmyard enclosed on three sides by stables and out-buildings.

'Jump down, Raoul,' said Mr. Birk, 'and walk up to the house. I'll meet you there. I'll see to your suitcase.' He pointed with his whip behind his shoulder. Raoul Marek turned round and was speechless. Behind a vast semicircular gravel space, on which stood a colossal lime tree, he saw a wide and towering mass of stone, spreading into square and irregular wings on either side, with a square tower and many turrets, and with three rows of small windows beneath the crenellated battlements.

'Not a bad old place, eh?'

'I don't know what to say, Mr. Birk. It's fantastic. I don't know how to express it.'

Ten minutes later, with Mr. Birk leading the way and accompanied by a man with the suitcase, he was climbing a circular staircase and following him through a passage which led in a straight line along the whole length of the second floor.

'That's your quarters, young man; at least, I think that's the room my sister wants you to have. We don't hire it out often; what with the barred windows, it gives people the creeps; but there is my niece to come with her husband, and what with one thing and another, just haven't got the rooms.

You'd think we'd have no end of guest rooms in this place, wouldn't you, and so we have, but they are empty, most of them. Just can't afford to have them furnished. Still, this is a nice and sunny room you've got; it used to be a nursery once.'

'Is that why the windows are barred, Mr. Birk? Very wise, I think. Very good idea, with small children.'

'Lord no. I had that grille put in years before, on the doctor's advice. This was my wife's bedroom, you see. She was melancholic. Always talked of committing suicide. I always said it was stupid to make all this fuss to guard her. If people want to kill themselves, let them, if it gets as bad as that. And it didn't stop her, of course. She took an overdose of sleeping drugs in the end.'

'How terrible for you, Mr. Birk.'

'Well, I don't know. We've all got to die, you know; can't live for ever. Now come and look at the view. Don't get that in Prague, do you, eh?'

The view was enchanting. Behind a flagged terrace with a moulded balustrade and set with white stone urns lay a rose parterre arranged in neat scrolls and ovals round a baroque fountain with a shallow basin and the figure of a cherub. This was bordered by stepped-up banks of grassy slopes linked by white stone steps, and beyond it lay the park – immense and inscrutable.

'There's a pond over there. You can't actually see it from here. It's got an island with a pavilion on it, but don't try and see it, because the bridge is falling down. Otherwise you can roam all over the place. It takes two hours to do a round of the park. So there's some nice exercise for you. Now I suppose we'd better get down to my sister. If you want to wash you'll get some hot water brought up. You just get out on the landing and yell. There are no bells either, you see. Hope that bed will be all right for you. You are small and light, you'll be all right in it.'

'What a beautiful bed, Mr. Birk.' It was the only good piece in the room, a narrow directoire bed with yellow and black bands of inlay on the curved ends.

'Well, I don't know about beautiful. I once sat down on it while my man was pulling my boots off and it collapsed under me, haha. Now let's go downstairs, shall we?' He went to the bedside table and tapped against the blue enamel candlestick. 'Remind them to give you a candle tonight or you'll be sunk.'

CHAPTER 3

'MAMA, EMMA has just told me that a case of pineapples has been delivered. She asked me for what occasion they were meant, and there I stood and looked a fool. I wish you'd tell me about things. Nobody ever tells me anything.'

'I am sorry, Alice. It had slipped my mind. I ordered them as soon as we got the post card from Luzern,' said Mrs. Birk-Borovec and looked above her daughter's head.

She was seated on a French settee whose arms and back were decorated with black and golden sphinxes behind a small table of satinwood, with a pack of patience cards on it, with a roll of crochet work on her lap and a book by her side. She held herself very upright as was the custom of her generation, contemptuous of slackness of mind and body, a generation whose ideal had been embodied by 'Franz Joseph, our Lord and Emperor', the monarch who used to get up in the Hofburg at five every morning from his iron camp-bed covered with common army blankets.

'I am not – criticizing you, mama. But I always try to cut down expenses – you know I do – and I save a crown here and five crowns there, and then you let yourself go with

28

your extravagances. I could weep when I think of it. I could howl, I assure you.'

'Nobody could live more frugally than we do, Alice.'

'I know, mama. And I understand really. It's because of – I know. You were quite right. I am sorry, mother.'

'Don't fret yourself, Alice. We know that your intentions are always the best,' said the old lady with a sigh.

Alice ran her fingers along the windowsill to see if it had been dusted. Then she stepped back and moved about the room restlessly, adjusting a vase here, an ashtray there, and straightening a cushion. After having been widowed for a second time she had made her home with her mother, and although everybody in the family regarded this as natural, she smouldered with resentment of being dependent on the old lady, and tried to appease her own conscience with dreary self-imposed tasks which nobody demanded. Her vitality, which had been a charming vivacity in her youth, had grown into an unpleasant craving for activity, of 'making herself useful', as she called it, and had sharpened her handsome features while preserving her girlish figure, which made her look much younger than her forty-two years.

'I fear young Marek has arrived, too,' she remarked now, looking at her mother with a frown. 'I'd better go and see about his room; I'm sure nobody else has dreamt of raising a finger about it. Really, mama, I often think your place would go to rack and ruin if I was not about. Not that I mind working hard – you know I like it. Though I wish Bettine would try and make an effort as well. But one can't shake her out of her laziness. The house could be on fire and she wouldn't move a step faster.'

'Don't worry so much, Alice. We are doing very nicely now. I had another talk with the agent and he is quite satisfied.'

'So long as we keep on living simply, Mama.'

Although Alice chided her mother from time to time about 'extravagances', she was as convinced as the old lady that their way of living was extremely modest. In the pantry there were shelves filled with pots of *pâté de foie gras*, but it was home-made. Two hundred cows stood in the sheds, but cream with tea and coffee was only served for important visitors. Sheets and tablecloths were never purchased when the need arose, but linen was bought from Ireland, by the bale and unbleached, and was whitened on the lawns in summer and later on cut up and hemmed in the sewing-room. Flour, coffee and tea, raisins and almonds were ordered by the sack at wholesale prices and kept under lock and key by Alice. Twice a year Alice and her younger sister Bettine acquired model dresses from Paris from one of the best dressmakers in Prague, but all their other clothes were made by a seamstress who had visited the family for the past twenty years, and who spent a week or ten days in their house about every six weeks. They took a box in the State theatre for the whole winter season, but would have considered it extravagant to buy an odd ticket for a play at another theatre. There was an abundance of womenservants, but they would have thought it pretentious to keep a butler. Neither of the ladies ever dressed their hair themselves, because they were groomed by their maids, yet a visit to a hairdresser in town was only allowed for important parties or balls.

'I've been thinking, mama, if young Marek gets poor Helen's room, then Margot and Oscar can have the blue room and use Margot's old room as a dressing-room. They give on the park, and then they can't complain about farm-yard noises.'

'That's splendid, Alice.'

Alice fingered the doorknob and gave it a twist. 'Mama,' she said resolutely, 'what did you make of the post card?'

'Really, Alice, what am I to make of it? One does not pour out one's heart on a post card, you know. And even if other people did, Margot is the last person who would.'

'Yes, she is very reserved. Not the way Bettine is reserved, who just doesn't open her mouth, but reserved in a chatty sort of way. She babbles like a brook. But never about what you want to know.' She paused. 'Do you think she is happy, mama?'

'You are expecting too much, Alice. Happy, happy. Who ever is? Have you ever been happy? Has Bettine? Has any-body you know?'

'I don't like it, mama. If at least she would open up.'

'You always want to get to the bottom of things, Alice, as though it helped. You remember your Uncle Karel. He always said: Alice isn't curious; she only wants to know.'

Her daughter gave an irritated laugh. 'That was about the only funny thing he ever said. I suppose they'll have children sooner or later, and she'll love them and settle down. A bit of love, that's what is lacking.'

The old lady glanced at her sideways. 'The way you talk, Alice. Always a schoolgirl at heart. Love, love! Heaven for-bid. With Margot, I mean. You have a loving heart yourself and are always willing to make sacrifices. But your daughter was not made that way. She is ambitious now and I'm thankful for it, because it keeps her going. Oscar is rich and it flatters her, and so far so good. But if love came into it – and neither Oscar nor children would arouse it, I assure you – she would be reckless.'

'I suppose you are right. And it cannot be undone any more. Although I often wish—— Of course, I am to blame, mama, and Uncle Tony, too – although he wouldn't hear of it. We are all guilty, mama; we pushed her into it.'

'Nonsense, Alice. She did not need much pushing. Oscar's millions did it quite effectively. And we have a lot to be thankful for. We wouldn't be sitting here now if it hadn't been for Oscar, and Margot is having a good time and plenty of amusement. And that is what she is after, all said and done.' The old lady gave a sigh and picked up her crochetwork and silently unrolled the ribbon of lace at which she worked.

Alice remained by the door and looked at her mother with a mixture of hatred and resignation. As usual during their conversations, she had been cut short and dismissed. This stout old woman with the thick white hair and the smooth white face, the broad brow, the heavy eyelids and the double chin, had something so statuesque and dignified about her that even the closest members of her family did not dare to interrupt her silences.

Alice shrugged and left the room.

A few moments later she was back with her Uncle Tony and Raoul Marek.

'I am glad you have come,' said the old lady to the guest,

and after laying her needlework aside, she gave him her hand, which he kissed. She put a few questions about his parents and his brothers without seeming to listen to his answers.

'We are going to have coffee in a minute, Mr. Marek,' said Alice. 'We are only waiting for Bettine to come down. I think you'll want it after your journey. Although perhaps at your age you are not so dependent on it. It's peculiar, the older I get, the more I want my coffee at regular hours. It's a sign of old age, I'm sure.'

He made a perfunctory protest.

Emma, the head parlourmaid, entered and surveyed the company with the contempt of the impeccable servant.

'The coffee will be ready in the saints' room, madam,' she informed Alice.

'Oh, Emma, I had thought it would be nice to have it in the octagon room.'

'Not in that heat, madam. I had the blinds drawn ever since morning and it still is like an oven in there.'

'Very well then. And send up some of the almond cakes.'

'Not today, madam. They are still too fresh. They would give Mr. Tony indigestion.'

'Have you told Miss Bettine?'

'She is coming down this minute, madam.'

Emma retreated after this almost daily skirmish, in which she nearly always was the winner and which the old lady was always careful to ignore.

The door opened again and Bettine came in.

'This is my younger daughter Bettine – Bettine, you remember Mr. Marek?'

'Of course I do, mama. How are you, Mr. Marek?'

33

She was a tall and buxom young woman of thirty, fair-haired and pale. She had the same smooth face, broad forehead and heavy eyelids as her mother, and it was obvious that at a more advanced age she would grow stout. She had also inherited the dignified bearing, but what in the old lady was natural and imposing had changed in the younger woman into the frozen calmness of very shy people and the do-not-touch-me attitude that tries to ward off any potential hurt. She was not married.

Raoul had met her several times in Prague, at dinner parties and receptions. He remembered her beautiful manners and her distant air. She danced badly and always kept in the background. Although nice-looking and beautifully turned out, she was not attractive to men and was always praised by other women as 'so extremely ladylike'.

'Aha, here she is. No wonder she does not dare to show her face. Come here, young woman, I've got a bone to pick with you. Aha, she's blushing. I should jolly well think so.'

'I don't know what you mean, Uncle Tony?'

'Don't you, now?'

Mrs. Birk-Borovec rose. 'If you please, Tony. We are going to have coffee now.'

'Suits me all right, Ida. Coffee or no coffee. I'm going to have it out with that daughter of yours.' He trampled behind the ladies, keeping a painful grip on Raoul's arm.

As soon as everybody was seated, Emma poured out the coffee at a side table and handed it round, while supervising a young maid who served cherry sponge and small croissants filled with poppy seeds and chopped nuts.

Alice pulled out the skin formed by the hot milk on top

34

of her coffee and made a face. 'It is disgusting, mama. This skin is enough to put anybody off. How often have I told them downstairs that the milk must be only heated and not boiled. But, of course, nobody ever listens to me.'

'Give it to me, Alice; I like it. It's the best part of the milk,' said the old lady.

'Don't you think it's disgusting, Mr. Marek?' clamoured Alice.

'Now, don't you frighten young Marek, or he'll bolt from the room and run straight back to town,' shouted Uncle Tony. The young man did not know what to say and helped himself to more cake than he really wanted.

'Now, as I was saying, Bettine, you leave that horse alone next time. Prochazka saw you feeding her with handfuls of green grass.'

'But Melody liked it, Uncle Tony.'

'Aha, so you admit it. Now, that she liked it is no excuse. If she has no more sense, then you should have it. That's what human beings are here for, to know what's good for a horse and what isn't.'

'Yes, Uncle Tony, I'm sorry.'

'No good being sorry, my girl. Nobody wants you to be sorry. You've done it and you admit it and that's all there is to it. You'll know better next time, eh? I never go round snivelling when I have done something. If I do it, I do it; that's good enough for me and anybody else. If I have to face the music afterwards – well, what of it. A decent person always takes the responsibility for their actions; that's what makes them decent. And I've never regretted a damn thing in my life. What do you say, Ida?'

'I daresay you haven't,' said his sister and dipped her cake into the coffee.

'There. That's the way to be, Bettine. Head up and the world belongs to you.'

'Yes, Uncle Tony.'

'We are all jolly decent people here, young Raoul. You got into good company. Hasn't he, Ida?'

'If it pleases you to think so, Tony, all the better,' answered the old lady.

'What do you mean, Ida? Do you mean we are not, or what?'

'Let it go, Tony.'

'What the hell does she mean?' thought Raoul. 'She does give queer answers.' Everything was queer. He wished he had obtained more information about the Birks before arriving in Kirna. He felt slightly offended that nobody attended to him and that they continued with their family banter as though unaware of his presence. On the other hand, he was grateful for it, because it gave him more freedom to puzzle things out. Were they really so rich or were they penniless? He looked up at the ceiling covered with a baroque painting of saints who were writhing on fat clouds, clad in billowing garments. Their pink limbs, held in agonized attitudes, were so arranged that they pointed towards the central medallion, forming a star. After he had contemplated the splendour, his eyes travelled down the walls, which bore faded traces of frescoes which in turn were abruptly cut off by a band of coffee-coloured oilpaint. The old parquet floor was partly covered with strips of linoleum and the remnants of what had once been good Persian rugs. The chairs were of wicker-work. There were rickety flowerstands of bamboo and carved shelves of walnut. The big table was covered with a stiff damask cloth with a coat of arms woven into it. Some of the appointments were of old-fashioned silver and the sugar bowl of pressed glass had a tarnished lid held by a broken hinge. His attention returned to the table talk. They were discussing the illness of one of the kitchenmaids. Mrs. Birk-Borovec had been nursing her for the past three days, giving her drugs and applying poultices. Now she had recovered.

'Mr. Marek, don't you think that mama is a saint?' asked Alice. 'She did simply everything for the girl. She is wonderful that way, you know.'

'Not at all, Alice,' said her mother dryly. 'If you don't stand over them they don't take their medicine. That's all there is to it.'

'My God, she is businesslike,' thought the young man. It did not occur to him that there was the contrast between two ways of living. Alice, the younger generation, had already been reared in town and was inclined to view everything with a sentimental eye. The old lady had been born and brought up on the estate, and she knew that it is no act of charity if the farmer helps the cow to calve, or ministers to the sprained ankle of his helper. Animals and people alike have to be kept fit.

After a few more minutes of local talk, Mr. Birk stated that he had to go over some accounts and the party broke up. The old lady was going to play some music and Bettine offered to come and turn the pages for her. Alice proposed a walk in the park to Raoul, but in the same breath advised him against it, as the heat was too great. 'After dinner or early tomorrow morning,' she concluded. He was glad enough to retire till dinner-time.

When he entered his room he found there the little maid who had handed the cakes round at table. She was putting the last of his belongings into the drawers of a chest, and he saw that she had rolled up his ties. He took them out again and told her to hang them in the wardrobe.

'There's nothing for this, sir.'

'Well, hang them over the back of a chair and put my suits away and then you can go.'

'Where am I to put your suits, sir? I've put the one in the wardrobe already.'

'Well, put the others there, too. Or is that too complicated?'

'It's not that, sir. But there's only the one coat-hanger.'

'Well, bring some more. Let me see. Only three more.'

'I can't, sir.'

He was more curious than annoyed. 'Surely you don't mean to say that in a place like this you don't have any spare coat-hangers?'

'We have, sir. But, you see, Miss Margot and Mr. Oscar are coming tomorrow or the day after, and all the hangers have been put in their rooms, and if I gave you some of them now, I'd only have to take them back again tomorrow.'

'But come, what is three coat-hangers? Hang it all! They've probably got twenty.'

'More than that, sir. But it would never do for me to interfere. Mr. Oscar has to have everything just so, and if anything came out Mr. Tony would be that angry. He'd rather go without anything himself than let Mr. Oscar go short.'

'All right. Fair enough, I suppose, although I don't see it.'

He gave her a five-crown piece which she took with a curtsey and tried to kiss his hand, but he stopped her.

When she had gone, he took his shoes off and walked up and down the room in slippered feet. He was not angry, but more bewildered than ever. He knew Oscar Ritter vaguely. He had not seen him since his marriage to Margot, but he had always struck him as an unpleasant person, a typical businessman with a permanently preoccupied air. As far as he knew, Ritter relished farm life and the stables as little as he did himself, and he thought it most unlikely that a man like Tony Birk would put great store by him. Yet there it was. 'Perhaps it is for the young girl's sake,' he said to himself. Still, it was doubtful. His mind went back to the coat-hangers. Nobody seemed to consider him. Nobody had talked to him at table, except when appealing to him because of some of their incomprehensible family squabbles. They certainly had not put themselves out to entertain him. Why had they asked him to come? He had known the reason before setting out, but now after his first experiences he felt very dubious. His father had made a fool of him. Bettine had not spoken to him once. Although – that was understandable. Perhaps she was just as embarrassed as he was.

He looked out of the window. The steps spread from grassy terrace to terrace like a fillet of satin and behind the baroque fountain the trees stood in a bluish-green mass. The rose trees had straight stems and well-rounded crowns and were sparsely set with pink and red flowers. They were pruned and trimmed to the last leaf and twig. He shook his head. The upkeep of the park alone must be costing a small fortune.

He sat down on the bed and wondered if his father had not been right after all. . . .

CHAPTER 4

MRS. BIRK-BOROVEC was standing by the grand piano in the octagon room and putting away the sheets of music she had played during the afternoon. It was a constant wonder to her family that she played so badly, although she was extremely musical and still sang occasionally with a voice which had lost some of its volume, but nothing of its youthful sweetness. Often people hearing her sing in an adjoining room had taken it for granted that it was the voice of a young woman.

She had changed from her grey linen dress into one of grey foulard. Ever since her husband had died fifteen years ago she had worn black in winter and grey in the warmer season of the year, a perpetual mourning which was not so much the outward sign of her grief as a comfortable way of settling the cares of her wardrobe. She took care with her appearance, dressed in a stately manner, and had her hair done in an old-fashioned and elaborate way, not because she was vain, but because she felt it was her duty to do so.

There was a slight knock at the door and as she called 'Come in' Raoul Marek came into the room, followed by

Emma and a maid who was carrying a tray of glasses, a decanter of sherry, and a silver platter with salted almonds and cheese biscuits. The little maid stopped by the door.

'Where would you like the drinks, madam?' asked Emma. 'In here or in the drawing-room?'

'Leave them in here, thank you,' said the old lady.

The little maid advanced, breathing heavily and amid a violent clatter of glasses, till Emma took the tray from her without a word and carried it on her white-gloved fingertips to a table in complete silence. This display of virtuosity pleased the young man.

As soon as the servants had left, he said: 'I say, Mrs. Birk, that parlourmaid of yours is rather wonderful, isn't she?'

'She is. What one calls a jewel.'

'I suppose she has been with you for ages?'

'Not so very long. Only – eight years. But you see, she has to keep up her position here – she has to be excellent. She is not from our part of the world. She comes from the Sudetenland. The German cleanliness and efficiency, you know, and that strong self-respect. She is a complete stranger among the girls we have here, and if she wasn't superior to them, where would she be? She has to keep herself apart, whether she likes it or not. Would you like some of this sherry, Mr. Marek? There is whiskey and gin, if you'd prefer it, but you'll have to wait till my daughter Alice comes. She keeps it locked up. It gives her something to do.'

'I shall be delighted to have some sherry, if I may. Can I pour you some?'

'That would be very kind of you.'

'That maid of yours. She came and told me that I needn't dress. That's all right, is it?'

'Quite all right, Mr. Marek. We never dress unless we have big parties.'

'I was really impressed with her. The ideal servant, you know. Just when I was wondering what to do.'

He filled two glasses with sherry and carried them to the grand piano. 'And very good-looking really. So tall and blonde and carries herself so very straight. I am amazed that she is still with you – I mean that she hasn't got married.'

'That type never does, Mr. Marek. She is an intelligent person, as you have seen yourself, and ambitious into the bargain, and has a strong feeling for quality. She has gone almost as far as she can – she might go into service in an aristocratic house later on – but that would be the end. She has grown out of her own class. The men who might marry here are not good enough for her; her standards have changed too much. And you should see her on her day out – in a tailor-made and a fox fur – she would pass anywhere. It's a tragedy really. Ambition is not a very good thing, Mr. Marek.'

'Oh, I don't know. We all want to get on.'

'Get on to what, I ask you? To the brick wall against which we hit our heads?'

They fell silent and sipped the sherry. Raoul crunched a salted almond. He felt very hot.

'Still – I mean – you don't have to be ambitious,' he began. 'You are very lucky. To own a place like this. I had no occasion to tell you before, but I was startled when I saw it. It's so beautiful that it is quite unreal somehow. This room, for instance – it's magnificent.' He indicated it with a sweep of his hand.

'Yes, it is rather beautiful,' said the old lady complacently. It was a vast octagonal room with three uncurtained french windows leading on to a long balcony. Each wall was covered with a painting of a Tyrolean landscape, executed with the brittle charm of the rococo. There were hills crested with ruins, pine woods and waterfalls, meadows with mountain brooks whose water flowed in curly waves, and flocks of sheep guarded by shepherdesses who held beribboned staffs and baskets of tumbled flowers. A few carved and gilded chairs, placed along the walls, looked too spindly to be ever sat upon. The three blue plush fauteuils drawn round an inlaid ebony table looked more secure. The music stool, now occupied by the old lady, a white and gold music cabinet, and several round and crescent-shaped tables which had been gilded once, completed the furnishing. It occurred to Raoul that the flimsiness and shabbiness of these pieces did not really matter. It was a room which one could not kill and it would swallow any type of chairs and tables with the greatest unconcern and without losing by it.

'I've only seen photographs of that sort of landscape decoration before,' he said. 'I never dreamt I should ever come across it in real life.'

'We've had it photographed, as matter of fact, by an architectural paper,' said the old lady. 'And this is not all,' she added with a smile. 'We've got another celebrity in Kirna, a tree. You shall see it tomorrow. We had a person from Kew Gardens here last summer to look at it. It flowers once every forty years and there are only two other specimens in the whole of Europe. At least, so he said. Anyway, it did not flower while he was here. It should have done, but it didn't. One can't have everything all cut and dried.' She looked pleased.

'I say, you are lucky. I'm not really surprised, though, because the park looks like a fairy tale, just what I've seen from the window.'

'I am glad you appreciate it,' answered the old lady. 'I like people to give praise when they think it due. I always think it is a sign of mediocrity if people do not feel any enthusiasm, and if you don't allow yourself to be impressed you condemn yourself. It's the essence of provincialism. The man from the provinces never laughs at a joke and never admires anything.'

'Yes, I've always felt that myself,' said Raoul. He dipped his fingers into the almond dish and found that there were only two almonds left.

'I'm awfully sorry. I've been a pig. I've eaten the whole lot,' he said. 'I never noticed it.'

'Don't worry, there are plenty more. It's really Emma's fault. She puts everything into tiny bowls, because she thinks it's more polite.'

For the first time in the day he felt completely at ease.

'That's what I always feel,' he started. 'There's nothing wrong with the provinces except that they are so terribly provincial.'

He was rewarded with another smile and a quick glance from beneath the lowered eyelids. He was almost sorry when Mr. Birk joined them. He had discarded his breeches and was now clad in a string-coloured gabardine suit with big flaps on the pockets, somewhat suggestive of a military tunic. His feet, although not booted, made as much clatter as before.

'Aha, that's how I like it. Getting drunk on the quiet and never a word to other people that there is some drink to be had. Well, young Marek, you young tripehound, are you going to give me a glass? Woa, not too much. I've just had a spot of tiddley with the agent, in that miserable kennel of his. I'm quite happy for the time being. He's not a bad fellow. Really, Ida, he isn't.'

'I never said he was, Tony.'

'Well, nobody ever said so. He's all right. The way he's managing the accounts. My eyes popped out of my head. Still, just as well, because Oscar will want to see them. And I could have never done anything like it, mark my word. He's really worked hard. Not like you young gentlemen, lounging about in your offices with a cognac and a paper and killing time till you can go and see your chorus girls, hahaha.'

'You are being very old-fashioned, Tony. They don't go in for that any more.'

'Don't they? Well, they are damned fools, that's all I can say. A nice girl from the ballet, all curls and giggles and as plump as a partridge – I've never gone in for that slimming craze, my boy – I don't like needles.'

'Spare us the details, Tony.'

'Why should I? I've nothing to be ashamed of. Now, what have you been up to, young Marek, apart from sozzling and and trying to make a good impression?'

'He has admired the room, Tony,' said the old lady quietly.

'Glad to hear it. Funny thing that, you know. We never

45

knew we had it till only about ten years ago. There was a wallpaper on it, from the times of the parents, you see, all grapes and leaves and things, not very fetching – still, I suppose the parents liked it. Anyway, we had it torn off and wanted to have a plain paint on it or something, and one of the workmen scratched at the wall and discovered all that glory by accident. Funny, isn't it, when you think what we might have missed. Still, I'm damn glad we've got it; it's impressed young Marek, and that's the main thing. We can lift our head again, Ida; he approves of us, haha.'

Raoul Marek felt at a loss at what to say. He cursed the old man, who seemed so stupid, and yet seemed to divine his thoughts.

'Have another drink, Raoul, there's a good fellow.'

'Thank you very much, Mr. Birk.'

They heard a discreet cough at the door and perceived Emma.

'If you please, madam, the ladies cannot find the big bottle of lavender water.'

'It's in my bedroom, Emma; you know where. On the second shelf in the small cupboard.'

'We've looked everywhere, madam. Perhaps madam would like to have a look herself.'

The old lady glanced at her sideways. 'Very well, I'll go – and bring some more salted almonds in the meantime. You'll excuse me, won't you?'

Once outside she turned to Emma. 'The ladies are in where?'

'In Miss Bettine's room, madam.'

Mrs. Birk-Borovec passed the landing with a quicker step

than usual and entered her daughter's bedroom. Bettine was sitting in front of the dressing-table, fully dressed, with her hands in her lap. Looking at her in the glass the old lady saw that she had been crying.

Alice stood slightly behind her to the right, wringing her hands with an exasperated air.

'Mama, don't you think that Bettine is ridiculous,' she began. 'Can't you make her change her dress? Thank God, I came along to look at her before dinner. She will put on her old red when I tell her she looks a hag in it, and she's got the nice green one in the wardrobe and the white and the new tie-silk. But of course, as soon as there is a young man in the house she makes herself hideous.'

'She looks very nice, Alice. I don't know what you want.'

'Well, I do and I shall say so till my last breath. It's no good closing your eyes to it. I've just told her if she never takes any trouble she'll never get anybody worth while looking at her. If she'd listened to me more we would have married her ages ago. Why, at her age I had the men falling over themselves and I would have them still if I lifted a finger. But there she is, always lounging about in a corner and never opening her mouth. And I can't run after her in front of people and make her pull herself together. I made signs to her this afternoon to talk a bit, but no, there was nothing doing. I could weep, mama. I really could. I could howl.'

'Why can't you leave me alone?' said Bettine with a voice smothered by sobs. 'I know all about your admirers. Ten on every fingertip. Well, be glad of it and shout it from the rooftops, but leave me in peace.'

'No, I won't leave you in peace. I won't, I tell you. Do

you think I enjoy myself running after you and telling you that you look a sight? Now, here, for instance; just look, mama, the way her hair stands out at the back. Nobody else would notice it, of course. You can thank the Holy Virgin on your knees that you've got me, Bettine.'

'Leave her now, Alice,' said the old lady 'I'll see that she does her hair properly. Not that there's much wrong with it, when I come to think of it.'

'There you are, mama, always pandering to her. If it wasn't for me, she would look like a scarecrow. I never had such round shoulders when I was her age and I still haven't, thank God; but then, I take exercise and lead an active life. If she'd only listen to me. But she makes no effort. No wonder she frightens the men away.'

'And if I was a man, you'd frighten me away,' said Bettine in a very low voice. Her eyes were blazing.

'I think you'd better go, Alice, and entertain our guest,' said the old lady. 'And send Masha in on your way and I'll stay and supervise her. She is still a bit raw.'

'Raw! Of course she's raw. Where should the perfection come from. If Bettine would kindly deign to train her a bit, it would be a very different matter. But of course, everybody expects me to do everything the whole time. Nobody ever bothers to do their duty.'

She tore out of the room and banged the door. She would have been deeply offended if anybody had told her that her actions were not prompted by her sense of duty, but by very different motives.

The old lady took a chair, placed it next to her daughter and sat down with a sigh.

48

'There, Bettine,' she said. 'Take a few deep breaths and wash your face with eau de Cologne.'

They remained silent. Bettine attended to her face and then began to comb her hair hastily, with the nervous movement of people who know that they are gauche and resent being watched because of it.

'Don't tear at your hair, Bettine. You've got such nice hair. You should be kind to it,' said the old lady.

'Mama,' said her daughter. She spoke with difficulty, as she had put two hairpins between her lips. 'I sometimes think Alice would like to kill all people who have not got good figures and who don't keep their shoulders back. Sometimes I am afraid of her. I really am.'

'We must make allowances for her. She is an unhappy, restless soul. Now, dinner will soon be ready and we'll all feel much better afterwards. There is nothing like food.'

'What do you think about Marek, mama?'

'Just a little social climber, my dear. The type who has got good manners, but only when he thinks it worth his while. He'd probably slave-drive the servants if he had the chance, but kill himself to carry a small parcel for a lady. He'll come in useful when Margot arrives. I like having young people about for her sake. He will amuse her and be harmless. That type never has the guts to break up an existing arrangement. He is quite happy to sit and purr at other people's fireside and share their dishful of cream so long as he has not got to pay for it.'

'I am glad you say that, mama. I agree with you. But Alice is already scheming fiercely.'

'Don't take any notice of her. You know the way her mind

runs. Either you are married and then you've reached the supreme goal, or you are not and then you must try and achieve it. Now, come along; we must not let them wait.'

'I'm coming, mama. Just my handbag. Can you see it anywhere? I could have sworn it was on the bed.'

'It is, Bettine.'

'Ah, just like me, not to see it. But that's what I can never understand about her attitude, mama. Why does she want everybody to be married, when all the married couples we know are unhappy, and her own two marriages have not been so wonderful, either? She should know better by experience, I should think.'

The old lady rose. 'Now, have you got everything? Your bag and a handkerchief? That's right. I am afraid I can't give you the answer. Of course, I could say that she is a flapper at heart and all that, but that would not be quite right, either. I should say because she lives, and because all life is stupid, and because it is this very stupidity that makes life go on and on. And I am too old to care any more. Now you'd better turn the lamp down.'

CHAPTER 5

'BETTER LATE than never,' said Alice as her mother and sister entered the octagon room. 'Still, I always feel, Mr. Marek, that it doesn't matter how long a woman takes over her appearance, so long as the result is good. Don't you agree?'

He bowed. 'How could I not agree in the face of such radiant evidence.' He bowed in Bettine's direction without seeing the look of embarrassment and contempt she gave him.

'May I press you to a glass of sherry?' he added.

'Yes, thank you very much.'

'I hope you don't mind the way we are sitting in the twilight, Mr. Marek,' said Bettine and began to sip her sherry. 'You see, so long as there is no light in the room we can keep the windows open. But once the lamp is lit we have to close up, otherwise we would be smothered by gnats and moths.'

'I don't mind in the least, I assure you. I always think that dusk is the most attractive hour of the day. And this background is made for a sort of Götterdämmerung, if I may say so. Not teutonic Gods, of course, but something delightful, eighteenth century, I should imagine.'

'Mama was quite right about him,' thought Bettine as she listened with an approving smile. 'Only I wish he'd learn to climb with a bit more polish. Twilight being attractive. Attractive. And then Götterdämmerung. Dragging in his good education. Still, it would go down very well with most women.'

'I must apologize for dinner being so late,' remarked Alice. 'But it's through no fault of ours; it's really an act of God, so to speak.'

'Well, for heaven's sake, Alice, don't apologize in that case. Can't stand apologetic people. Never could. Hang it all, why can't you say: Dinner's late, folks, take it or leave it; if it's good enough for the Birks, it's good enough for most people. And anyway, what's that act of God you are babbling about? If you ask me, I have a shrewd idea that it's that stinking oil lamp again and not so much of the Almighty. What do you say, Ida?' and Mr. Birk sat down heavily in one of the blue plush chairs and looked inquisitively at the old lady, who was bending over the music-cabinet and sorting out a few sheets of Bohemian songs.

'I am always so sorry for moths, aren't you?' asked Bettine. 'They are so ugly and soft and clumsy and they don't do anybody any harm.'

'You are quite right; I always feel the same,' assented Raoul.

'I am inclined to agree with you, Tony,' said the old lady while she turned over a bundle of sheets with slow and careful fingers. 'I always feel God should be left out of things as much as possible, although he comes in very useful at times, of course. If you have sinned and are punished, you have been chastised; and if you are innocent and have been stricken, then the calamity was sent to try you.'

'Aha, aha. Jolly good show. I knew you would support me. Did you hear that, Alice?'

'I did. Of course, mama will have her little jokes. I don't know what Mr. Marek will think of us. He will think we are a Godless household.'

'Not at all, I assure you,' replied Raoul. 'But what is this I hear about the lamp?'

'It's an eternal curse,' said Alice and tugged at her string of pearls. 'It's the big oil lamp we have in the dining-room. It's a hanging lamp, attached to the ceiling, you know. And sometimes – not often, of course – but very occasionally, it sheds a lot of soot all of a sudden; we have never found out why. It rains down black particles and dead flies and moths, all on the freshly laid table. And the whole dinner-table has to be relaid and a fresh cloth spread out – that's why we are so late tonight.'

'I don't mind – not in the least – but don't you believe this rigmarole, young Raoul. It happens at least twice a week. As regular as the calendar!' boomed Mr. Birk. 'And I always say we should have candles at dinner; damn it, that's not asking for such a lot, is it? But no! Oil lamp it has to be. But I wash my hands of it.'

'You are very unfair, Uncle Tony,' said Alice. 'You don't seem to realize – but then men never do. It would take about two dozen candles to have that table properly lit. It would be simply burning money. But I am quite used to it, of course, by now. Always reproaches about this and that, but no thought whether it would be economical. It's a very ungrateful task running a house, Mr. Marek.'

'Nobody's reproaching you, Alice,' said Mr. Birk. 'All I said was: lamp – dirt, candles – no dirt, hahaha. I'm not laying the table, so I don't mind, hahaha.'

'More sherry, anybody?' asked Alice, biting her lips and straightening the string of pearls round her throat. 'You seem to be having quite a morbid conversation over there, about moths and being sorry for them. Two young people like that, I would have thought you'd find something more cheerful to talk about. When I was young and pretty——'

'When you were young, you mean, Alice, hahaha.'

'I was always full of fun. Although I never approved of that silly giggling, mind you. And there are many serious things in life, of course, and one can't always be joking. I learnt that only too soon. And once one has entered into life, one is not the same again. Something breaks inside you. Although I've always believed in pulling myself together.'

'Good old Alice. She is a sport, isn't she, young Raoul?'

'I am sure she is, Mr. Birk.'

'Doesn't take offence at anything I say. That's the way to get on with me. Can't stand all those namby-pamby people and milk-and-water misses that are being turned out nowadays. Why, if a girl is as squeamish as that, what good is she to anybody, I ask you?'

'Let it go, Tony,' said the old lady. 'We are not disputing what you say.'

'There you are, young Raoul. You see the way they try to damp me down. I've got the reputation of being a profligate.

And all this because the other day I came up behind one of the maids and she dropped her tray and broke the whole blasted coffee-set on it and then she said that I had tickled her. It's her mind that was tickling her, not I. I didn't dream of it. She'd never occur to me, the little slut. Now, if I had my choice, it would the agent's wife, although she is a bit queer, but I would not mind that. Now, she's the real goods, if you ask me!'

Emma appeared, heralded by a knock and a cough. 'Dinner is ready.' She swept the room with a contemptuous glance and then hastened forward to help Mrs. Birk-Borovec with a grey woollen shawl which she draped over her shoulders.

'I'll help mother with this,' said Alice impatiently. 'You would be much better occupied to look after the table. I'm sure that Mila is slopping the soup all over the rim of the plates again.'

'It's cold soup tonight, madam, and I had it served in cups.'

'I see.' Alice's glance travelled slowly and malevolently over the parlourmaid's face and figure. The cap sat straight and firm on her head with every frill prinked to shiny crispness. The ash-blonde hair was drawn back from the face without a wisp straying. There was no crease or stain on the black crêpe dress and the tiny muslin apron was attached at the front with a plain golden pin. There was no fault to be found from the white cotton gloves down to the black patent leather shoes fastened by a strap and button.

Alice sighed. 'Are you ready, mama?' she asked.

CHAPTER 6

THE DINING-ROOM was quite large, but not huge as Raoul Marek had expected it to be. It had a green and lemon striped wallpaper with groups of miniatures on it and a high vitrine filled with old Bohemian goblets and cups, with thin Copenhagen tea cups, with an old Dresden coffee-set gilded and strewn with flowers and the carved ivory busts of some royal-looking personages on ebony pedestals; all the pretty junk that accumulates in a household, that is never broken because it cannot be used, that cannot be given away as a present because it might be recognized, and that is not thrown away because it might have some value.

There were two fine walnut chests in the provincial French style, covered with lace mats and beset with cheap glass fruit dishes. In one corner of the room stood the life-size bronze of a Savoyard youth with a flute and a marmoset in his arm, and in the other a copy of Rodin's 'Thinker' on a base of black marble. There was a smell of fresh bread, meat broth and burning oil.

'At last!' shouted Mr Birk among the general scraping of chairs. 'I hope it's been worth waiting for.'

'You behave as though you had not seen any food for the last three weeks, Uncle Tony,' said Alice with restraint. She added: 'If we get through the meal without any more accidents, Mr. Marek, perhaps you would like to take a turn in the park afterwards. I am sure Bettine will be pleased to take you. She needs exercise, you know, and I am always glad of anybody who encourages her to it.'

'You'll be all right, so long as you don't go near Crete or the Jordan, or you'll be bitten to death by the gnats.'

'Quite so, Mr. Birk.'

'Uncle Tony, how on earth is poor Mr. Marek to understand you?' said Alice with a tone of sweet reproachfulness. 'You see, Mr. Marek, we have got quite a little language of our own. We are such a united, happy family and we have all our little secret jokes and it must sometimes be trying for an outsider. Crete is a small island on a pond. I believe it was given the name during the war of liberation in Greece – I am not sure myself – and the Jordan is a deep well under a sort of stone hood. It is rather creepy; nobody knows how deep it is and we don't know what spring feeds it. Because even in times of the greatest drought the Jordan remains unchanged. Bettine will show it to you; it is under the sweet mulberry tree.'

'And one more thing before you are let loose, young Marek,' said Mr. Birk. 'You've got the run of the place, of course. Whatever fruit or flower you fancy, you just pluck it. Only whatever you do, don't touch the roses. You can have roses, of course; if you want a bunch, say so. But don't cut them yourself. We've got a gardener who does not like anybody to cut a rose. He cuts them himself if you wish it.

Got the idea? He's a deuce of a gardener, though. Getting on to eighty and still going strong. He'll show you all sorts of things if you get round him in the right manner. And the way he treats the flowers – you should see him at it; it's a regular bedside manner he has with them, more like a doctor dishing out medicine. What do you say, Ida?' He chuckled.

'Really, Uncle Tony,' said Alice.

'The never-ending source of amusement,' said the old lady and glanced at him sideways.

'I wish I could understand half of what they are talking about,' thought Raoul Marek. But whatever was irritating about the conversation was richly compensated by the food that was served. There had been iced clear meat soup with pastry triangles filled with liver, followed by potato pancakes with a ragout of mushrooms, after which came roast veal speckled by strips of pickled cucumber and bacon and surrounded by bone-marrow dumplings and cream gravy and accompanied by a green salad with a crown of hard boiled eggs. At present they were eating curly squares of fried batter with a wine sauce, which in this part of Bohemia is called 'God's mercies'.

'And another thing before you go out, Mr. Marek,' said Alice, 'in the future when you stroll about alone, don't go beyond the raspberry bushes in the kitchen garden; that is, not after sunset. You see, there is a sandbank behind the thicket with a bench on it and lavender and thyme and camomile – rather pretty. The agent's wife goes there every day at nightfall, when it is fine. Don't ask me why, but anyway, she goes and sits there and she does not like to meet people. We never go near the place. It is ridiculous, of course – we have as much right to it as to the rest of the grounds – but it is an act of courtesy on our part, you know. Not that I believe in pandering to people, but she is definitely queer. I am really very sorry for her. Although I think she could pull herself together. If we all let ourselves go like this, Mr. Marek, where would we all be?'

'I don't really think that she is unbalanced,' said the old lady 'She is oversensitive and very shy, but I don't consider it queer if somebody does not like his fellow creatures There is something most appealing about her, something that tears at your heart strings.'

'Mama is a saint, Mr. Marek; don't you think so? The way she talks about that woman. Actually, I would not mind her being so eccentric if she was not so stuck up. One day my mother had the carriage ready to go to Brandys for shopping and she met Mrs. Holub – that's her name – and asked her to come along with her. I would love to come, said Mrs. Holub, but I am not properly dressed. I am not properly dressed either, said my mother; we don't bother about hats and gloves and cloaks here, you know. So Mrs. Holub, if you please, answered: That be as it may, madam, and it does not matter in your case, but with me it's different, because I've got something to represent.'

'I can quite see her point, Alice,' said the old lady. 'We are in her eyes above reproach; we are the owners and anything we do is becoming. But she feels herself to belong to the small fry and knows that as such she will be readily criticized. She is very particular about what is fitting and what is not.'

'I suppose she is, mama. And do you remember last year, when she had the same dress as I? It was an accident, of course, although I cannot understand how she can afford that dressmaker – still, I dare say she saved up for it for two years – anyway, there it was, the same stone-grey crêpe and the same cut down to the last button. And as soon as she saw that I had it, too, she packed her dress up and sent it back to Prague. It would never do, she said, to wear the same as the lady of the castle. Silly goose.'

'I think she was perfectly correct, Alice,' said Bettine. 'And she is not so shy as all that. I sometimes meet her during daytime in the garden when she comes out to pick up a lettuce for lunch or a bunch of radishes, and she is always most pleasant. She is just so terribly sad.'

'Margot is very fond of her,' remarked the old lady. 'You will see as soon as she arrives she will be over in the cottage for at least an hour. When she is here she goes and visits her every morning.'

'I wish I could,' said Mr. Birk. 'She is as pretty as they make them. Eyes like velvet and deep lashes, set in with a smutty finger, as they say. And always so trim with that curled fringe on the forehead and tiny hands and feet, like made of marzipan.'

'She is pretty in an old-fashioned sort of way,' said Alice. 'But her airs and graces are quite ridiculous. You should see her when she goes to Podebrady to the Spa. She goes once every week and Prochazka has to drive her in the closed coupé. Even in boiling weather like this. There she sits in that musty old box on the smelly blue velvet cushions and he has to put a fresh flower in the silver vase; it's all fitted out very well, you know, Mr. Marek, with cut-glass appointments and little mirrors and things, very *ancien régime*, you see. And she sits inside and draws the curtains, so that nobody can look at her, I suppose – quite like the Empress Elisabeth – and holds on to the silk strap whenever they go round a bend. You've never seen such a performance.'

'And she rides side saddle; she looks most picturesque, Mr. Marek,' added Bettine. 'I hope you'll see her one day. A long dark green riding habit and a hat with a dripping feather. I don't know how she keeps it on; I would lose it after the first canter.'

'She rides damn well,' said Mr. Birk. 'And it's a pleasure to look at her, all in the old style. Sometimes I give her a leg up, not the way as with you girls, but I hold out the palm of my hand and she steps on to it as light as a feather. But always rides out alone. Keeps herself to herself.'

'Very much so,' said Alice. 'You would not believe it, but she keeps hens in her kitchen; between the double windows. The sill has been made exceptionally wide and there they are. She does not want them to get mixed up with our own poultry. Have you ever heard anything like it? As though anybody would begrudge her a chicken coop.'

'She has an awful life, though,' said Bettine. 'To judge from the little that Margot has told me. She has lost a son and never got over it, and her husband is awful. He never speaks a word to her. Not because he is nasty, you know, but he just can't be bothered. Sometimes when he says something, she asks him about it and he replies I was talking to the dog, not to you. It must be a horrible life, all alone in that house, mostly in the kitchen, of course, and no friends to see and nothing to look forward to.'

Fruit was placed on the table in an old silver epergne and a brown majolica dish. There were yellow Napoleon pears and greengages, large gooseberries, and those small deep red apples which ripen earlier than any other kind.

Mr. Birk picked one up. 'Hold it to your ear and shake it,' he said to Raoul Marek. 'And you'll hear the pips move about inside. They are quite loose when they are ripe.'

'Can I peel a pear for you, Mr. Marek?' asked Alice. 'Or do you really want one of these apples? Wouldn't you think Uncle Tony was five years old, the way he rattles it about? Still, I don't mind a bit of fun even when it is a trifle childish. But when people play about with apples at Christmas, it always gives me the creeps. I don't think it is funny at all, do you?'

'I am afraid I don't know what you mean,' answered the young man. He thought: 'How is anybody expected to know what they get up to at Christmas.'

'It's a very old Bohemian custom,' explained the old lady. 'I dare say it is pre-Christian, like so many of these Christmas beliefs. And, of course, it is only practised in the country, like all these superstitions.'

'You see, it's like this,' broke in Alice. 'Everybody takes an apple from a dish, choosing it himself. Then the apple is cut in half horizontally and the core with the pips comes up like a five-pointed star. Because an apple always has the core in five partitions, you know. If your cut apple reveals a star then you are all right and will live. But sometimes by a freak there is a cross instead of a star and that means that you will die before the year is out. Very silly, really.'

62

'Does the prediction ever work?'

'I don't know. I can't remember that anybody ever got a cross in their apple and I suppose they died just the same. The only time was last year; Oscar had a cross and he is still alive, of course.'

'But the year is not yet finished, Alice, hahaha.'

'Oh, don't be so silly. I don't believe that sort of thing is a matter for joking, do you, Mr. Marek? There are subjects which must be respected.'

'That's all schoolbook rot, Alice,' said Mr. Birk. 'And you had better get on with that pear for Raoul. He won't get fat on respect, will he? I have seen too much to care one way or the other. When I was in the Serbian campaign I saw the fields littered with the lights and livers of the men and there was nothing very sacred about it. I think we make too much fuss about human life. It is not as valuable as all that. Hang it all, you can always sell this and that, you can get a price for a cow and a hen, but nobody will ever pay a crown for you, will they?'

'Oh, you are hopeless, Uncle Tony.'

Afterwards, when Bettine and Raoul Marek went into the park, the young man said: 'I do enjoy your uncle, Miss Bettine. There is something so refreshing about him.'

'Yes, I suppose so. Shall we go past the rose beds and across the lawn? I propose we go down the chestnut avenue and I'll show you the old oak and then we turn back again; it will be too dark to go any farther.'

'I shall be delighted.' He offered her a cigarette, which she declined.

'I admire him,' he continued. 'He does not mind what he

says, does he? Always frank and makes no bones about his opinions.'

'That is quite true, Mr. Marek. But then, you see, it has been easy for him. He has always lived on the estate, always his own master and had never to bow down to a superior. And in the Army they used to encourage this spirit, too. The brotherhood among officers, you know. Or perhaps you don't know, because now it is different. But in the Imperial Army, I was always told, the officers had to say "thou" to each other. The youngest subaltern thou'd the oldest general. It makes for an air of equality, I think; every man as good as the other.'

'I quite see your point, Miss Bettine.'

They had passed the rose parterre and the main part of the turf. Now they walked more slowly, as the grass grew high and thick around them, with tall marguerites, sorrel, butter-cups and dandelions.

'We get lots of dog-violets round here in spring,' said Bettine. 'And beneath the trees there are lilies-of-the-valley and wood-anemones. But, of course, they are over now.'

'It's delightful. There is such a profusion of everything. Even the weeds are luscious here.'

'Yes, that is because of the dampness, Mr. Marek. The whole park is so damp; that is why there are so many gnats.'

They approached the chestnut avenue. The path lay in the dark grey evening mist, while swarms of midges moved above their heads like billowing veils. The sky was pale pink, sparsely strewn with deep pink clouds, but as soon as they stepped beneath the trees they were shut off from the rosy light.

64

'Are you sure you will not smoke?' asked Raoul Marek. 'Even if it is only to keep away the things that fly through the air.'

Bettine shook her head. 'So long as you go on with your cigarette, we should be fairly safe. Be careful how you step. Sometimes there are already some chestnuts on the ground and they make you stumble. They will soon be ripe. In another fortnight, I imagine. Margot loves chestnuts, you know. When she was a child our gardener used to make little men for her with matchstick legs, or carve them into mushrooms and baskets. Nowadays when she comes down in autumn she still insists on having her baskets and mushrooms made for her. She is not really grown up. Or perhaps she is. She is a mixture, I suppose.' She laughed quietly.

'You are very fond of her?' he ventured.

'We all are. We can't help it. Of course, we don't see a lot of her nowadays; they are living in Prague the whole time, you see – I mean Margot and her husband – and they don't come down very much. A week here and there, perhaps. They have just been abroad for the last six weeks, France and Italy, and returned through Switzerland. And now they are coming to Kirna for a week or so, as a sort of rest cure, I dare say.'

'It sounds lovely, Miss Bettine.'

'Yes, it sounds lovely.'

'I have only seen your niece once or twice,' continued the young man. 'But I have a very charming memory of her. Though a bit wild, as I remember. It was at the Weinzettel house, I think; we played going round the room without touching the floor. Could she climb! And really she enjoyed herself. Not like the others, who were simpering or thought it too silly for words.'

'Yes, I can just see her doing it,' said Bettine. 'Of course, she would not do that any more; she is more sedate now. That is, when she is in Prague. When she comes here, it suddenly falls away from her and she is all over the place like a whirlwind. Although I think it's natural. Kirna means all her childhood to her.'

'And to think that she still plays with chestnuts. She must be very softhearted and – and like a child.'

'Yes, she is that,' said Bettine with some hesitation. 'But then – I don't know. She is moved very easily, you know. And softhearted, as you said. But then, the next minute she can be quite ruthless – ready to walk over corpses, as the saying goes. Of course, she is very young. She will get more even later on, I think.'

They were at the end of the avenue. In front of them lay a small clearing with a flat-roofed building, only big enough to hold one room, and an oak tree grew next to it. It seemed to the young man that he had never seen a larger tree before.

The sun had gone down and a pale crescent moon stood in the slate-coloured sky.

As they moved nearer he drew his breath in. He saw three small barred openings without panes.

'This is very strange, isn't it?' He turned to Bettine, keeping very close to her. 'These iron bars – I thought at first that it was a lodge or gardener's cottage – the light is so dim. But it cannot be. Was this perhaps a summer-house for Mr. Birk's dead wife? He told me about her this afternoon. I am in her room, you know.' He gave an embarrassed laugh.

66

'Oh no, nothing of the kind,' answered Bettine. 'This house, or whatever it is, has never been lived in as far as anyone can remember. We have not been in Kirna so very long, really; my great-grandparents bought it – and we don't know much of its history. They acquired it from two old spinsters of the nobility, I believe; they were the last of that branch. There are some rusty chains and locks inside the place. It was either used as a prison in the old days or perhaps as a place for monkeys or other wild animals. In the eighteenth century it was very fashionable to keep exotic beasts.'

'Yes, that's the explanation,' cried Raoul Marek. 'I am quite relieved you know. It rather gave me a shock – I believe it would give anybody a shock, coming upon it so suddenly. Although it was foolish of me to imagine anything. One's imagination runs away at times. Now, when I come to think of it, I don't know how I ever could imagine that your uncle imprisoned his wife here – it's really too funny for words.' He took a white handkerchief from his breast pocket and mopped his face. 'Silly of me,' he muttered. 'And your uncle is so very kind. A bit rough on the outside, but so jolly really, and a heart of gold. Could not hurt a fly.'

They did not move. Her face was pale and her eyes were very dark. Her lips were half open in a smile.

'He is rough and jolly, as you say, Mr. Marek,' she said slowly. 'But a heart of gold. Really! How long have you been practising the law?'

'Not very long. Only for the last two years.'

'I thought so. And you have not done lots of trials, have you? What I call the human stuff?'

'Not really. That is more my partner's side. I go in for more technical things. Drawing up of contracts and financial advice.'

'There. I knew you had not had much experience with human nature. No, Uncle Tony is not what you would call kind. He is very good-natured and easy-going of course, but that is different. He is good-natured so long as he can afford it, so long as it does not cost him anything. You see, at heart he is a fanatic, and like all fanatics, he will not allow anything to stand in his way.'

'You amaze me. He – a fanatic? Why, he clings to the past regime of course – but then, this is only natural for his age.'

'Oh, it's nothing political I meant. He has one great love, and that is Kirna.'

'But that's quite natural, Miss Bettine. Anybody who owned a place like this would be in love with it.'

'Yes, but he goes too far.' She paused and wetted her lips. 'I don't know why I am telling you all this, Mr. Marek, but then, it is always tempting to shatter innocence – well, anyway, I won't say anything about poor Helen; she was a bad case of melancholia. But he had three children; two boys who are living in Prague now. And there was a daughter; she was a beautiful girl. Rather like Margot in temperament and classical features. It was a pleasure to be in her company. She started lung trouble when she was seventeen and it did not look too good. The doctors advised Switzerland for at least two years. If only she would get over twenty, they said, she would be past the danger-line. In those days we were hard up, Mr. Marek. I know a big estate like this always looks prosperous – the corn grows and the sheds are full of cattle – but that is very deceitful. It is always difficult to raise liquid money suddenly, and in those years the farm worked with a heavy loss. The cane sugar dominated the world market and the beet prices were too high and the beet could not compete. There it was and there was the sick girl, and these mountain sanatoriums cost a fortune. Uncle Tony would not borrow money from Max – the brother who lives in Semtin – because he had only just bought him out of his share of Kirna; he did not want to show that he had bitten off more than he could chew. A part of the estate was mortgaged already, so he could not raise any money that way. There was only one thing to do and that was to sell some fields or a part of the forest; he was indignant at the very thought of it. His daughter stayed here and got consumption. She was gone in six months. It was heartbreaking. One does not know what might have happened otherwise. She might have died, too, or she might not. But certainly, any other parent would have given her all the treatment available.'

'That's terrible, Miss Bettine.'

'It is to us. Not to him, of course. We are doing quite well now, I think, as far as I know. But if the same thing happened, he would do it again.'

'But surely, your mother – she is part owner, too, isn't she?'

'Yes, she is. But nothing can be changed or sold unless they both consent to it. And after her death her share goes over to him, or if he dies, to his boys.' She gave a short laugh. 'I dare say then they can start all over again. But this should not surprise you. There are always quarrels in families over property. It would be a miracle if there were none.'

69

'Certainly, Miss Bettine. As you say, it would be a miracle if there were none. You have such a shrewd way of putting things. I admire you for it, if I may say so.'

'Do you?' They moved a few steps forward. 'I should have thought it would have chilled you. Men don't like shrewd women, as a rule.'

'They don't. You have hit the nail on the head again. Not the majority. But I am different. I look upon these things differently.'

'Ah, yes. You are different.' She sounded weary. 'And this, Mr. Marek, is the famous oak tree. Nobody knows how old it is. Some say at least five hundred years, but it could be up to a thousand.'

'How very fascinating. The whole park seems to be full of riddles.'

'Yes, one might say so. You see, it's propped up with a metal beam on this side. And if we go round to the other side, you can see the statue.'

'Another surprise. This is wonderful. Of course, the trunk is so thick, I would have never suspected anything.'

The bark was almost black in the growing darkness and looked more like a twisted monument of granite than wood. Some of the powerful branches were leafless, but a good half of them were richly covered with foliage. The statue was almost hidden in a niche formed by a curve in the trunk. It was a woman seated on a throne; she had a broad and strangely smiling face with blurred outlines and a crown on her head. Her arms and feet were placed in rigid symmetry. A circlet of thin gilded tin was attached to the points of her crown.

'This halo is, of course, fairly recent, about fifty years old or so,' Bettine told him. 'We don't quite know what she is, either. The people hereabouts call her Saint Anna, but I am not so sure. I think she is a Bohemian pagan goddess of fertility or something. She is very old. It is too dark now, but in daylight you can see how dark the chiselling has become. And she was not always here, either. There is a story that she was somewhere else on a crossroads and that she was carried here afterwards.'

'How extraordinary,' remarked the young man. 'Everything is so strange here. I am not surprised that you love this place.'

They proceeded towards the castle.

'You might call it love – or worse than love,' said Bettine slowly. 'It is difficult to say where love stops and obsession begins. Probably we cling so much to Kirna because we are comparative newcomers.'

She paused for a while.

'When Uncle Gustav was born – that was a younger brother to Max and my mother and Tony and Louise – he is dead now – he fell in the war – when he was born, Uncle Tony was eleven years old. And he tore up some sheets with rage. Because he knew that there was another brother with whom he would have to share the property.'

'I cannot believe it – a child of eleven?'

'Yes. It is not a very pretty story. But true nevertheless.'

It had become night. The rose trees stood black against the dark blue sky and the water in the basin glimmered with the reflection of the stars. There was light in a few windows and in the octagon room on the first floor a yellow glow illumi-

71

nated a patch of the painted landscape. It seemed as though a low-burning lamp was placed at the very end of the room. Despite these signs of life, it was difficult to imagine that the castle was inhabited. They ascended the shallow steps which curved towards the terrace in an outline of broken scrolls. Behind the balustrade was a group of garden chairs and iron tables and on one of them a cluster of nets.

'Look at the hammocks,' said Bettine, pointing towards them. 'They should have been taken indoors for the night. It is too late now; they are already soaked with dew. If you like to, you can have a hammock put up tomorrow. Where-ever you wish it.'

'I should like that very much. Then I can imagine that I am floating on a green sea. Or no, I shall not imagine anything. It will be afterwards, when I am away from here, that I shall pretend that I am still in Kirna.'

Their footsteps echoed across the terrace. Raoul Marek felt that he had been talking nonsense and was also annoyed with himself for clattering so loudly over the flagstones. It unnerved him to have thus to listen to his steps.

'I should think that you would hate to live anywhere else,' he ventured.

'I don't know. We should not like to be here in winter, you know. Uncle Tony stays, of course, and I think mama would not mind so much, because she was born and bred here, but even so – we would not relish it. No hot water and very bad heating and the lamps which always give trouble. But once it is fine we don't want to be anywhere else. I never miss the town. I don't like parties and people very much. I like my peace and quietness and being left to myself.

And then, it is such a comfortable feeling to be somewhere where everybody knows you for miles around and accepts you for what you are and you don't have to be more sociable and pleasant than you want to be. They look on you as they would on a tree or a beet; you have been planted there and nobody will criticize you.'

'She is a born old maid,' thought Raoul Marek, and that was more or less what Bettine had intended him to think.

'I suggest we go upstairs and see what the others are doing,' she said to him. 'And perhaps there is still some of the Graves left over from dinner. I feel thirsty, don't you?'

'I should like a drink,' he agreed.

They met Emma in the passage with an eiderdown quilt over her arm and behind her the little maid with her arms full of blankets. She stopped.

'There has been a telegram, Miss Bettine, from Miss Margot. She is coming tomorrow with the three-five. She will be alone. Mr. Oscar is stopping in Prague for a day or two.'

'Oh, good,' said Bettine. 'I am so glad she is coming. It is a pity, of course, about Mr. Oscar.'

Emma gazed into the distance with her correct blonde head held high and remarked: 'That is so. Now, if you will be good enough to excuse me, we must be getting along.'

'But, Emma, you are not going to start getting the bedroom ready at this time of the night.'

'I am, Miss Bettine. I don't hold with too much sleep. It makes one heavy and dull.' Her glance travelled eloquently over the little maid who was standing nearby, round eyed and open-mouthed.

'I suppose you are right, Emma. But don't overdo it.'

'Nobody has ever died from overwork yet, Miss Bettine.' After another look in the same direction, she moved away.

'My God,' said the young man. 'That Emma of yours. She does keep them in order.'

'Very much so, Mr. Marek. Sometimes it makes me uncomfortable. But she is very decent and has a great sense of justice. There are never any revolts.'

'I don't think anybody could rebel,' answered the young man. 'She has something so determined about her. It must be wonderful to have someone so absolutely loyal and devoted about.'

'It is a nice feeling, I agree. And she seems to stick to us. Margot would give anything to have her, but she will not go. And yet she dotes on Margot.'

'Amazing, isn't it?'

'Not so much once you know the set-up.'

He glanced at her, but no explanation followed.

CHAPTER 7

IT WAS on the following morning at a quarter to ten, when Alice, Bettine and Raoul Marek assembled at the coffee-table. The breakfast-room was on the ground floor and separated from the hall by the gunroom. At this time of the day it was delightfully sunny and appetizing; the dotted muslin curtains were as white and frothy as milk, the bird's-eye maple wood of the furniture was light brown, crisp and glossy like fresh rolls and honey and the light blue cushions suggested a clear summer sky.

'What an inviting place,' he said.

'I am so glad you like it; we all do,' answered Alice. 'Uncle Tony uses it as a dining-room in winter, because it is easy to heat. There is nobody else to come down now. Uncle Tony has had coffee ages ago and mama has hers in bed. How do you take your coffee? Half and half?'

'No, almost black, thank you.'

'That is very bad for you, isn't it, Bettine? I always think strong coffee for young people is poison. I never allowed Margot to drink any until she was twelve years old and even then she drank it very weak. She used to be quite cross at the time, but I always said: You will grow up one day to thank me for it.' She handed him his cup and began to butter a roll.

'The coffee is pretty bad, Alice,' said Bettine, who up to now had been silent. 'Don't you think so, Mr. Marek?'

'It is – not very strong,' muttered the young man and took another sip of the chicory brew.

'It is perhaps a bit weak,' conceded Alice. 'You see, our cook can't really make decent coffee. Good cooks never can make coffee or boil eggs. And then, at breakfast she always makes it weaker than in the afternoon. And it's all very well for you to complain, Bettine, but you would never dream of going downstairs and seeing after things yourself.'

Emma entered with a pot of jam and a silver basket in which the hot rolls lay wrapped in a napkin.

'Ah, here you are, Emma. Put it down here. Mr. Marek, would you like an egg? I think it is very bad for you to start the day with a lot of food inside you, but please do have an egg if you feel like it.'

After Raoul Marek had declined the offer, Alice turned to the parlourmaid again: 'Now look, Emma, I don't want to go into the kitchen just now, because cook is on edge, but I rely on you to make absolutely sure that all the copper pans are put away. Mr. Oscar is not coming for another day or so, but it is better to play safe.'

'They are hidden in the scullery and they will stay there,' said Emma. 'They are beautifully clean, though. As if anybody wanted to poison him.' She pronounced the last sentence in such a contemptuous manner as though wanting to say that he was much too unimportant to be given so much attention.

Raoul Marek did not dare to ask any questions, all the more as he was not sure that he had heard right. He stirred his coffee at great length.

Alice threw an angry glance at Emma and said to the young man with a tense smile: 'My son-in-law is very particular, Mr. Marek, and very sensitive. Last time he stayed with us he had an eczema and he got it into his head that it was from the copper pans we are using. Of course, everybody knows that verdigris can be deadly, but our utensils are spotless, I can assure you, and besides, we were all in good health. He is much too intelligent, of course, to think seriously that anybody wants to poison him. I always tell Margot he does not really mean what he says; it's only that he is so strained and overworked. Bettine, your sleeve is in the butter.'

The young man looked at Alice, at her thick dark blonde hair, at the pointed face with the thin lips and the deep-set, restless eyes, at the embroidered lawn blouse under the yellow linen coat; and he wondered how much this well-groomed and embittered lady knew about her son-in-law.

Yes, he was quite willing to believe that Oscar Ritter was strained and, with added exhilaration, he told himself that the strain was due to more than a few tarnished copper pots.

He glanced at her again and hid a smile behind his raised coffee-cup. A nervous giggle rose in his throat. 'The famous Carlotta,' he thought. 'I wish I had met her. I wonder if she ever worried about Oscar Ritter's eczema in her time. Or perhaps there was no eczema then. Ritter was a few years prettier, as old Birk would say.'

77

His giggle grew stronger and he cleared his throat to hide it. He put down his cup and looked into it with a satisfied expression and for a hundredth time this morning he gloated about Robert's – his partner's – letter which he had received before breakfast. And for a hundredth time he regretted that he could not share the joke with anyone, not even with Bettine – although she probably knew a good deal about Oscar Ritter's past. How small the world was, he reflected, and what a treat for Robert to act as legal adviser to a beautiful woman. The famous Carlotta. He must write and ask him if she really was as beautiful as they said. Probably by now rather *passée* – these Italians faded quickly.

After the meal he strolled into the park, and thinking over what he had noticed on the previous day, it seemed to him that the castle held plenty of surprises and led one to expect – what did he expect? Things which probably had never occurred. His mood suddenly changed. There was always a harmless explanation at hand. The exciting never happens, he told himself. Nothing ever happens. A feeling of flatness and disappointment took hold of him.

He followed the same way which Bettine had led him the night before and then took a path to the right. He came across trees hung with tulip-shaped blooms of the colour of blood-oranges and a tree covered with white curly leaves which looked like the ringlets of a periwig. There were stone-oaks and other trees which he had seen in the Mediterranean and shrubs which flowered with the elusive pink of flamingoes and stretched scented boughs like fans towards the sky.

He did not know how long he had walked when he came

upon the well they called Jordan. He bent over the water; the stone hood shut out the light and he could not see his reflection. It smelled of depth and decomposition. He plucked two berries from the mulberry tree. They were yellowish white and tasted dull and sweet. He then ambled through a birch wood which spread over a hill behind the Jordan. The air was fresh and spicy there and he felt more at his ease. He wandered at the top of the ridge, tearing leaves from the branches which stood in his way and digging up with his toe the colourful mushrooms which grew between the tree roots. He picked up one, of a sickly white tint, and turning its stem between his fingers, saw that there were blue stains where he had touched it, like bruises on human flesh. He whistled defiantly and threw it away. He descended a ravine between clumps of birches and larch trees and saw at the bottom of the slope a brook running half hidden by willows and ferns. One bank was streaked with blue and yellow flowers and he jumped across the water and tore out a bunchful of them, with the roots. He followed a bend of the brook and found a clearing with two rusty iron cages on it. Their tops were domed and pointed like the onion-shaped towers of Russian churches.

A few steps away from them, by a group of shrubs which grew beneath a cedar tree, he noticed a crumpled-up rag of faded blue linen.

'So this is how they keep their park,' he thought; 'the rose-beds like drawn with a ruler and the devil take the hinterland.' The thought of it amused him so much that a nervous giggle rose in his throat.

He stepped nearer. It was not a rag. It was a man, an old

man in faded blue dungarees, in a queer hunched-up position, half kneeling, half squatting. A panama hat, large and sunburnt, lay by his side on the moss.

'I knew it, I always knew it,' said the young man to himself. 'A dead man. A tramp. No, a landed gentleman; they all look alike here. But I am not the least bit excited. I have waited too long for something horrible to happen.'

He stuck his flowers under one arm and with the other hand took out his handkerchief and wiped his forehead, and his neck. Suddenly the body rose and he looked upon a very old man, upright despite his advanced age, with weather-beaten, distinguished features and a short white beard. He stooped to lift up his hat, set it on his head, touched it with a finger and said: 'Good day, sir.'

'Good morning,' said the young man.

'I just had a look at the Japanese spice bush,' said the old man. 'If you want to, you can take a piece home with you. It's something special. It's not what you'd get every day.'

'I would like to very much,' answered Raoul Marek. 'Where is it?'

'Here, right where I stand,' and the old man pointed to a plant which looked like a dried-up, shrivelled bush, with meagre cinnamon branches and brownish leaves. He broke off a twig and crushed it between his fingers and held it under Raoul Marek's nose. It seemed to the young man that it exhaled the most alluring perfume he had ever smelt.

'This is incredible!' he cried.

'Gives you a surprise, doesn't it? And the whole bush is scented like this. Does not matter what you pluck, a leaf or a branch or the root.'

'How interesting. And it looks so – like nothing on earth,' remarked the young man.

'Ah, we have not got it all written on our foreheads what we are and how we are. And that's how it should be in life. If God had meant it otherwise, he would have sent us down to earth with labels. It's only in the Army that they swank about with their pips and stars. And if one of them goes by, you know here goes a captain or major and he earns so many thousand crowns a month. That's why the Army is wicked. The doctors think up new medicines and the soldiers think up new ways of killing. It's like gathering water with a sieve. They should hide themselves for their sins and not go about in their uniforms like peacocks.'

He produced a powerful looking penknife and continued: 'You had better give me your flowers, young sir; I'll trim them for you and they will be nice in your room. The roots must come off; they are no good to you and they will go back into the soil here and help the other flowers. There is a use and place for everything in life; we all serve a purpose, the humble and the exalted, and who is to say who is worth more?'

'I quite see your point,' muttered the young man. 'I say, you do it awfully well – I suppose you are the gardener?'

'The head gardener, young sir. Not much as it is and yet the head among the others who are still less.' He uncoiled a strand of bast from his pocket with the satisfied air of the man who carries all his wants with him.

'There, I'll tie it up for you; that's more like it, and there's some beech leaves with it to make it more dainty. Never put ferns with flowers; they don't go together. They are an older breed than flowers and they want to be kept by themselves.'

'I will remember this. Thank you very much. You must be very proud of the park. I have seen some wonderful trees.'

'Yes, they are beautiful. . . . But they are like a beautiful woman – a lot of trouble. Have you seen the sacred Chinese maidenhair tree?'

'No.'

'Ah, you passed it and you never saw it. It has leaves all in and out, if you follow. Have a look at it, young sir; it's on your way back, before you get to the chestnut avenue. When you stand in front of it, you stand on the threshold of life.'

'That's very interesting; thanks for telling me.'

'Very good, sir. I can't walk back with you; I have got to see about the crows in the coppice. But if you'll come in the kitchen garden in the afternoon, I'll show you a thing or two.' He touched his hat and was gone.

Raoul Marek made his way back to the castle with his nosegay swinging awkwardly from his finger.

CHAPTER 8

In the afternoon the family was assembled in the drawing-room, awaiting Margot's arrival.

Alice and Bettine were seated at a round table in the middle of the room. Alice was occupied with drawn-thread work on a square of lawn and cast her eyes from time to time on her younger sister, who was reading a book with both elbows on the table and her head in her hands, quite unconscious of the occasional reproachful glances she received from Alice.

Mrs. Birk-Borovec sat as usual, on the French settee with the black and gold sphinxes, and, as on the day before, she had her needlework on her lap, but did not touch it.

Her brother sat very upright on a chair by the window and read a copy of the *Horse and Hound*, which he held from him at almost an arm's length; he obstinately refused to wear glasses. He had been ordering this hunting journal from England for a long time, although his most recent visit to that country had been twenty years ago.

He spoke excellent English, easy and fluent, to his own amazement, as he himself always admitted that he had 'never been brainy'. If ever anyone complimented him on his achievement, he used to reply: 'Ah, it isn't what it used to be – I have gone rusty now; but in the years when I had my groom Robinson, it was a very different matter. That's the way to learn a language – in the stables, sir. Get away with your English governesses and misses. They sit at table stiff as a ramrod and all you get out of them, is – sugar, please – and – pass me the butter, please. It's a wonder they don't turn the milk sour. And if they are the riding kind, it's all the time: Look at this sweet cow – isn't it a darling? – and does not the lilac smell delicious?' Robinson, the model groom, had returned to his native country in nineteen hundred and fourteen at the beginning of the war, which was one of the reasons why, according to Mr. Birk, 'things have never been the same again'. It was especially at times when perusing the *Horse and Hound* and marking meets in the Counties of Sussex and Surrey with a pencil stub, for reasons best known to himself – that Mr. Birk developed a partly maudlin and reminiscent and partly aggressive attitude which was known among the rest of the family as the 'my-groom-Robinson-mood'.

Raoul Marek entered, halted at the door and took his thin gold watch from his breast pocket.

'Nearly four o'clock,' he remarked to nobody in particular. 'I dare say Mrs. Ritter will arrive any minute now. I think I arrived about this time yesterday, didn't I?'

'You did, I did, we both arrived together,' confirmed Mr. Birk from the window. 'But you see, we did not come here straight, we went to Semtin and took a look at the local types; so when you think of it, Margot should have been here already some time ago.'

'Of course, Mr. Birk, you are quite right. I should have thought of it myself. She should be here already, as you say.'

'That's what you think, young Raoul, always ready to agree and be pleasant and never another thought. On the contrary, it is quite natural that she is not here yet. Prochazka is driving her and once he falls asleep with the reins in his hands the horses walk till they are within sight of the park wall. If you consider this, then you'll agree with me that she won't be here for another ten minutes yet.'

'Definitely, Mr. Birk. Of course, I should have realized this.' The old man had made a fool of him again, and to cover the flush which had spread over his face, the young man stepped up to the table and sat down between the sisters.

'I don't know what it is, but I do know it is something very pretty you are making,' he said to Alice.

'Well, I don't know about pretty, Mr. Marek; you are very kind to say so. But it will be useful, of that I can assure you. A tray cloth, as you see.'

'Ah yes. By the way, I had a delightful, what shall I say – *rencontre*? – with the head gardener today. A very unusual type, I should imagine. A bit eccentric, don't you think?'

'We have got so used to him we don't notice it any more,' said Alice. 'And then, I don't feel it is necessary to chat for hours with the servants. Give your orders and be firm and brief and they will respect you all the more for it. Although, I must say I find it sometimes very hard to make a firm stand with them. They don't obey as well as they should. I know very well why, of course. Because I am widowed, a lonely woman without a man to lean on. Believe me, Mr. Marek, as soon as a woman loses her husband, nobody quite respects her any more. She is a shadow of what she used to be. And it is not only with the servants, it is in society, too. Why should people invite her and flatter her, when there is no influential husband any more by her side? The world is very cruel, Mr. Marek.'

'Damn it, Alice, the way you talk,' exclaimed Mr. Birk. 'And when you are in Prague, you are out every blessed day – afternoon and evening – it's nothing but parties and parties on end.'

'You are very unfair, Uncle Tony,' answered Alice and tore off a thread. 'That I am a widow and all alone in this world is not enough apparently. I have got to be punished as well for it by leading a life like a nun? Of course, nobody knows what I've gone through. Once you have lost someone near and dear to you, Mr. Marek, you are never the same again. I am not a woman of many words and I don't wear my heart on my sleeve, but I can assure you, something snaps right inside you.'

'I know that – of course I know it,' grunted Mr. Birk. 'I felt just the same when I lost my English groom Robinson.'

'Uncle Tony. I – I can't understand you. Sometimes you amaze me,' said Alice and stared at him with her hands sunk into her lap. 'I am really ashamed that I have to say this, but you force me to it. How can you possibly compare your feelings for Robinson with——'

'Why shouldn't I compare them, hang it all? When you have a good husband you are grateful and when I have got a good groom I am grateful. I can't see what's the difference. When I am fond of somebody I like him and I am not ashamed of it. It's the feeling that counts, the real feeling, and that's all that matters.'

'What did the gardener talk about, Mr. Marek?' asked Bettine and raised her head from the book. 'Did he talk to you about people going through life unrecognized?'

'Yes, that's right.'

'And then he brought in doctors and cursed the Army?'

'That was exactly it.'

'He always does it at the beginning of a new acquaintance, you know. Once he has established himself with his philosophy, he is more ordinary.'

'I actually wanted to ask you about him,' said the young man. 'There must be some reason for his behaviour.'

'There is, Mr. Marek. Did nothing occur to you?'

'I am afraid not.'

'I wish, Bettine, you would not drag out old stories which nobody wants to hear,' interrupted Alice and led the needle through the cloth with jerky movements.

'But please, madam,' said Raoul Marek.

'Very well then. But I think it's wrong. It is not that I am heartless and don't have sympathy with people, but there are occasions when it is proper to show pity and some when it is not.'

'He is a natural child,' began Bettine. 'Didn't you notice how distinguished he looks? His father was Count Torek, who was stationed in Brandys in those days with the Dragoons, and that is why he hates the Army so much. The Count married later on and settled down in Brandys and his son is Doctor Torek, our local doctor. Actually, we always think that our gardener looks more a nobleman than the

87

legitimate heir. You know what it is like in the country – everybody looks into his neighbour's saucepans and they all know who our gardener is. And naturally it irks him. That is why he is so insistent about it, that you can never tell the real worth of people and how everybody walks through life disguised, so to speak. It satisfies him.'

'But he seems to approve of doctors?' asked the young man. 'At least, if I remember rightly?'

'He does. He likes his brother. Some years ago Doctor Torek asked him to come and live with him in his house in Brandys – but he refused. He'd rather be our gardener. Although, perhaps one day, when he gets too old to be about a lot – he may yet accept the offer. He is already eighty-three.'

'We are all very fond of him,' said the old lady. 'And you can learn a lot from him. He has a great knowledge about the healing effects of herbs and all that. Once, I remember, Margot had a tooth pulled and it was very sore. Our gardener told her to rinse her mouth with camomile tea, but she would not hear of it. You and your old wives' tales, she said. Then she went to Prague to see her dentist and he told her exactly the same remedy.'

'How wonderful,' said the young man. 'If I am ever ill, although I hope I shall not be, of course, I will put myself in the gardener's hands.'

Mr. Birk rose suddenly. 'Here she is,' he said.

They all remained silent for a second. There were hurried footsteps and the sound and laughter of a shrill young voice. Emma's voice was heard answering. Then the door was wrenched open and Margot Ritter ran towards the settee.

She fell on one knee and embraced and kissed the old lady violently with the complete lack of self-consciousness of a child and also with the insouciance of the pretty young girl who knows that she presents a charming picture.

She was nineteen years old, and the elegant summer suit of blue silk edged with fox fur was too heavy for her frail and graceful figure. Her thick ash blonde hair, her large brown eyes and full, pretty mouth had an enchanting softness and bloom. 'Margot, collect yourself, not so much of a whirlwind,' said the old lady dryly, between the kisses, but the way she stroked her hair and looked down at her betrayed that she was moved. 'Get up, dear,' she added in a low voice. 'We are not alone. We have all been waiting for you and we have a visitor.'

Margot rose and smiled. 'How are you, mother? You look very well,' she said to Alice and kissed her quickly on both cheeks. 'And Bettine. And Uncle Tony. I don't have to ask you how you are; you look flourishing, as always, uncle. You will outlive us all yet; I always say so.'

'Shouldn't be surprised,' guffawed Mr. Birk. 'It's the good life I lead. Staying on my bottom, where I was meant to be, and not gallivanting about the whole time.'

'Margot, you are dreadful,' said Alice. 'But she does not mean what she says, Mr. Marek. It is only an old standing joke in the family. Margot, here is Mr. Marek, who wants to say how-do-you-do to you. You remember him from Prague?'

'Of course I do, Mr. Marek. How are you? Do you remember the party at the Weinzettel's? How we played mountaineering? I'll never forget your face when we hit you over the head and told you that you were so high up that you had hit the clouds.'

'Margot!'

'Oh, don't worry, mother. I don't do that sort of thing any more. I am a reformed character. Am I not, Uncle Tony?'

'Can't say yet. But still, I'll give you the benefit of the doubt, hahaha.'

'And how is Oscar?' asked Alice and folded her needlework.

'He is all right. I say, we have got a new stationmaster in Zelenec. A young and nice one. I have never seen him before? What has become of the old one?'

'He has gone into retirement, Margot.'

'Oh, what a pity; he used to be so nice. Do you remember every time we got off the train he would come to meet us and he'd say: The young lady has not washed her eyes today; they are quite dark.'

'I remember,' said Alice tartly. 'It's easy to make an impression on you. Anybody who flatters you, already as a child——'

Emma appeared in the door and announced that the coffee was served, in a softer voice than usual.

'It is in the saints' room, I suppose?' asked Alice.

'Are there any small almond cakes, Emma?' cried Margot.

'Of course there are; how would there not be, with Miss Margot at home? The coffee is in the garden-room, madam.'

'Oh, Emma, I am really annoyed. In this broiling heat,' said Alice.

'It's very nice and airy down there, madam – you get the coolness from the fountain, and then, Miss Margot likes it so much.'

'And I suppose that's why we've all got to suffocate down there,' replied Alice.

'Hang it all, Alice, if we have not slaughtered a pig, she might at least have coffee in the garden-room,' shouted Mr. Birk. 'Sometimes you hide your mother love so well that you take us all in, haha. What do you say, Ida?'

'I say that the coffee will get cold, Tony. And otherwise I say nothing.'

'But you think all the more, hahaha.'

'You will like our garden-room, Mr. Marek,' said Bettine as she rose and laid her book on the table, still open and with the back turned up. 'It is a sort of *salla terena*. Nothing as grand, of course, as the one in the Wallenstein palace in Prague, but very charming nevertheless.'

Alice rolled up her needlework with the quick prim movements peculiar to her and surveyed the table with a sharp look. 'Why don't you close your book properly, Bettine? It is criminal to put it upside down the way you do. You will spoil it for ever.'

'I have not got a marker and I shan't know where I stopped.'

'Ridiculous. You can remember the page.'

'I can't.'

'When I was your age, I had an excellent memory. I still have, thank God. Close the book, Bettine. It hurts me when people are careless with their things.'

Bettine had gone pale and her eyes had darkened.

'Do you hear me, Bettine? I shall not leave the room till you have closed it.'

'Shall I take your bag, grandmother?' asked Margot.

'That will be very nice. Let us go. I am not waiting for anybody,' answered the old lady. With a glance she compelled the young man to follow her.

'Now come along, both of you,' shouted Mr. Birk, and with each hand he took hold of Alice's and Bettine's arms. 'Stop the bickering, I say.'

'I am not bickering,' exclaimed Alice. 'How can you say such a thing!'

'Well, you are giving a very good imitation of it, haha.'

'You should know me better than that, Uncle Tony. I am only trying to do my duty.'

'Well, forget your duty for a minute and we'll all be more comfortable, hang it all.'

'It is all exactly as it used to be, grandmother,' said Margot in a low voice and took the old lady's arm. 'Nothing has changed,' she added.

Her grandmother looked at her sideways. 'Did you expect it to change?'

CHAPTER 9

THE GARDEN-ROOM lay on the park front of the castle. It opened on to the terrace through a curved archway supported by three pillars streaked with small-leaved ivy, so that sitting inside, the soft green and flowered parkscape was broken into four pictures, each framed by stone and foliage. The three walls were strewn with paintings of life-sized cockatoos, executed in the rococo manner. Most of the birds were cream coloured with sulphur crests, and a few were pale violet, pale green and turquoise. Clusters of leaves and pomegranates were set in the spandrils of the panels which enclosed the fluttering birds and above them curved the stucco ceiling moulded like a large scallop shell. The whole was not so much a room as a playful pretence of one and charmed by its undisguised artifice. A console table with a rose marble top and supported by a carved and silvered dolphin was flanked by two lyre-backed chairs whose tattered upholstery revealed the torn stuffing. In the centre of the inlaid marble floor a card table had been put up and set with cups and plates, and surrounded by a varied assortment of bamboo and wicker chairs. A small and rickety bamboo table was covered with dishes containing cakes and fruit tarts.

'It's lovely to be home again!' exclaimed Margot and clapped her hands.

While everybody was seated, she paced round the room, scrutinizing everything. 'Oh, good. There is still the moustache which Lolo drew,' she said and pointed at the disfigured face of the carved dolphin. 'But where is his cigarette?'

'Come and sit down, Margot, and stop being childish,' said Alice. 'I don't know what Mr. Marek will think of you.'

'But I want to know, mother. When the boys come over, they always give the dolphin a smoke. Do you remember, once on my birthday, they even gave him a cigarette-holder?'

'Margot.'

The young girl sat down with a pout. 'Really, mother. I have been away for so long, it's only natural of me to enquire about things. And I will have a drop more coffee, please; it is too light as it is.'

'Very well. You should not drink it so dark, but what's the good of talking; you don't take any notice of me, in any case.'

'But I do, mother. Every time I drink black coffee I have a guilty conscience and it makes it taste so much better.'

'That is at least something,' conceded Alice. 'Now have a cake. And then we shall want to hear all your news.'

'Well, everything was beautiful. . . . But very tiring. I really liked best the audience with the Pope. I wrote you about it. Oscar would not go, of course, because he said he would not kiss the ring with all the people before him kissing it and you don't know what filthy germs you pick up that way. So I went alone. It was unforgettable. And the Italian ice-creams are lovely. But in a way I think they are overrated. Berger makes just as good ices, I think.'

'I have always said you can't beat Berger,' Alice agreed. 'Even Rumpelmeyer in Paris is not quite so good. Nor Zauner in Ischl.'

'Aha, there you are,' said Mr. Birk. 'Might just as well have stayed at home. Your Uncle Karel was not so cracked after all.'

Amid the general laughter Raoul Marek turned to Bettine and begged her to explain Uncle Karel to him. He was told that Uncle Karel had travelled widely as a young man and when he got old had developed a passion for making speeches. All the children and everybody else who was in the house, including the servants, used to be called to his study and there he would start: 'You can be in Rhodesia, you can be in Queensland, you can be in Avignon, you can be in Bucharest' – and after enumerating thus places and countries for a considerable time, he would conclude with the rousing climax 'and everywhere it is the same'.

'We are, of course, very pleased to have you here, Margot,' said Alice. 'But I should like to know when Oscar is coming and why he stayed behind. It is just like you. A telegram and no explanations.'

'He had to have a look at one of the refineries and I don't know what,' replied Margot. 'And look into things for a day or two. He always thinks everybody is cheating him behind his back.'

'And do they, haha?' asked Mr. Birk.

'I am sure they would if they could,' retorted Alice. 'I understand this only too well. Your husband is a very wise man, Margot.'

'Yes, mother.'

'And when do you think he will be coming?' asked the old lady.

'On Sunday, for sure.'

'Oh dear,' said Bettine. 'And the boys are coming from Semtin.'

'That is very unfortunate,' said Alice. 'Couldn't we put them off? They never see eye to eye.'

'Oh, please, mother. I have not seen them for so long.'

'Hang it all, Alice, why shouldn't they come? They are good fun, and if a man of Oscar's age can't put up with a bit of ragging, it's just too bad. What do you say, Ida?'

'Let them come, Tony. The place is big enough to hold them all.'

Alice turned to the young man: 'Of course, Mr. Marek, it is not as bad as it sounds; I don't want you to think that there is anything wrong. We are all a happy family. It's only that my son-in-law is generally so preoccupied with business worries that it is difficult for him to relax. And young people can be very trying at times, when they are idle and run loose.'

'Stop worrying about what other people think, Alice, for heaven's sake,' broke in Mr. Birk. 'You always remind me of the governess whom Jenda asked to spend a night in a hotel with him and how she almost said yes and then backed out in the last minute because she was afraid of what the porter would think of her.'

'Uncle Tony, did this really happen?' cried Margot. 'I

don't believe it. He would never pick on a governess.'

'And why not, Miss Know-all?'

'Because he could not be bothered to plead with her for hours.'

'Could be. Quite possible.'

Alice said: 'Margot, you amaze me. I should like to know where you get this sort of knowledge from. Most unsuitable for a girl of your age, I can assure you. I really worry about you sometimes.'

Margot cast her eyes down and traced figures on the table-cloth. There were tears in her eyes.

Raoul Marek looked at the graceful throat, at the sweetly curved cheek, at the smooth eyelids. 'She is a still water, like her grandmother,' he thought.

CHAPTER 10

I<small>T WAS</small> ten o'clock at night. A strong wind had risen and the rustling leaves of the lime tree in the yard sounded like the murmur of a distant stream.

The dotted muslin curtains in the old lady's bedroom were flapping ceaselessly against the window-frame, hiding and revealing the green satin ribbon with which they were looped up, and alarming the moths flattened against the panes. The milky globe of the lamp brightened and dimmed with each gust of air and shed flickers of light on the brass bedstead, the black marble of the washstand and the blue-flowered china bowl, water jug and slop pail.

Mrs. Birk-Borovec lay in bed, propped up high by three pillows. Their starched frills made a stiff frame for her massive head and the thick plait of hair which fell over one shoulder. Her hands were folded over a book.

Margot sat on the bed, still fully dressed, but with her bare feet tucked under her. Her slippers lay on the floor.

'It is so nice here, grandmother. You have no idea how nice it is. I never really appreciated it before. And now it is too late.'

'If you come from time to time, you will enjoy it all the more.'

'Not really. While I am here, I think already of Prague and my life. Monday cleaning day, and Wednesday the washerwomen. What's the good of going to a theatre or to a party when you know that the next day you have to check the sheets and things will go wrong.'

'It should not be such an effort, Margot. If you have a good head housemaid, she can see to these things. Do you ever see me counting the sheets?'

'No, grandmother. But the servants always leave as soon as they are trained. I don't blame them, I wish – I often envy them. And Oscar overworks them terribly. He piles the jobs up for them and expects me to be after them the whole time. Already at breakfast it starts: Where is Anna? What is she doing? Where is Jean? You should know. You should give them a set time-table and see that they stick to it. You should know at any given time of the day what each of them is doing. And he thinks I should do more. And yet he is upset because I am so thin. Do you think I have lost weight?'

'Yes, you have, since I last saw you,' said the old lady.

'Oscar wants me to get stronger. Not for my own sake, of course. He thinks, I suppose, that I could do more supervising if I put on weight and were fitter. I always think it is a pity he did not marry my mother. They would suit each other much better. When we arrived the day before yesterday, it was rather late by the time we got home, and at midnight he wanted me to go down into the kitchen and count the good glasses, to see if any had been broken while we were away. I thought of mother then. She would have loved it. When I think how she locks up the sugar and the coffee and the liqueurs, she would be just the right woman for him. Although, she does it really because she has no proper work and it makes her feel important. And he does it because he really worries about his property so much. But then, of course, if he was not so careful about his possessions, he would not be where he is now. It has to be the way it is.'

'And did you count the glasses?' asked the old lady, without lifting her eyes.

'No, I didn't.'

'You had a row?'

'Yes. He went on and on for hours. How I don't share his worries and the least I could do would be to share responsibilities, and if I really loved him, I would do more for him, but that I did not care enough, and with his state of health I could show more consideration.'

'Is that why you came here alone?'

'Well, if you want to know, grandmother, it is. I had to have a breathing-space. He was cross at first and then he said that I could go, but if he was held up in Prague for more than two days, I'd have to go back again.'

The young girl rose and walked to the window, ruffling her hair and twisting strands of it round her fingers.

'You see, grandmother, that is the worst of it. He always forgives me in the end. And I don't. I can't. It is eating inside me the whole time. And of course, he is quite right. He does love me, and if I loved him, I would do everything for him and be more of a help. He always says he would not expect so much of me if he was not so fond of me. It makes me feel so guilty. He is really much better than I am; he has so many good qualities, grandmother, I always keep on telling myself.'

She stopped by the window and twisted a curtain and looked out into the night with unseeing eyes.

The old lady gave a sigh. 'It's as bad as I thought,' she said. 'Once you have to tell yourself the good points of the other person and find reasons why you should love him, it is not so good. Real devotion simply exists and does not ask why.'

'Do you think so, grandmother? I have never thought of it. But don't you believe that esteem and respect is a lot? Mother always says it is more lasting than love.'

'I don't agree with her. Esteem and respect and worthiness – it's a sorry business, Margot. Worthiness attracts boredom as surely as jam attracts flies. And what then? Boredom is the undoing of young people. First you are bored and then you resent and then it turns into hatred. Love does not last, but the other thing – is even worse.'

'I dare say you are right, grandmother. And every time I make an effort to be more the way he wants me, I get bad-tempered immediately again, because it is not natural to swallow reproaches and be nice on top of it. And it goes on and on. Already first thing in the morning I dread getting up – I know it sounds ridiculous – but I do, you know. I am so tired when I get out of bed. And he says: Why don't you look happy? You should radiate happiness; it's the least thing you could do, when I have so many worries. And I can't, grandmother. The more he says it, the less I can. He should know that one can't be bright on order. I am not a trained poodle, after all.'

'Get me my jar with the hand lotion, Margot,' said the old lady. Her hands were still beautiful; smooth and of an unnatural whiteness. While she spread the cream over them, she continued: 'You should do the same as I do, Margot. There is nothing better for your hands. One part of lemon juice, one part of glycerine, and one part of rose water. That is all the advice I can give you. I am sorry for you, but at my age, the only things I am sure of are recipes for lotions and cakes. Above that——'

'But why should you be sorry for me, grandmother? Most girls would envy me my marriage. And I know I am really very lucky. I am not unhappy, am I? I mean, you could not say that I was?'

The old lady drew a pair of kid gloves from beneath the pillows and put them on with slow movements. She did not answer.

Margot returned to the bed and sat down again. She held one hand up, to shield her eyes from the flickering light. She said: 'After all, what I was telling you, that's all trifles. Not big things. Unhappiness is when your husband drinks or betrays you or when a child dies. Real things, I mean. Don't you agree?'

'Have it your own way, Margot. If you say so, it is so.' She paused. 'And what am I to tell you? If you come back here, there is nothing much I can offer you. Do you want to live here and be bullied by Alice again? And where else could you go? You can't even make your own dresses or do any sort of work. That's not your fault, of course. But what life is there for you?'

'You are quite right, grandmother. It's all hopeless.' She

gave a forced laugh. 'And I don't know why we are talking like this, as though I wanted to leave Oscar. It would be sheer ingratitude of me; I'd deserve to be spanked for it. I would not be in my right mind if I even thought of such a thing. Not that I ever think of it, of course.'

She settled herself more comfortably and leaned her head against the brass bars of the bed.

'Life is very nice really. I don't know what came over me. I suppose we all feel depressed sometimes without any reason. By the way, grandmother – shall I put the jar away; you don't want it any more, do you? – I thought Marek was very funny. Mother wanted him to take a walk with Bettine in the park; you know what she is like, she wanted them to go all on their own, because young people want to be on their own, as she says. I went with them. She was annoyed, but she could not very well stop me. After all, nobody can say that I am not young. And he really amused me. He started paying me compliments and made himself so pleas-ant, and then he suddenly remembered that he was really supposed to court Bettine. So he pulled himself up and then he forgot again and was off again with me. And so it went on. He is silly, isn't he?'

'I don't care very much for him,' replied the old lady. 'It was Alice's idea to ask him to Kirna. She is always on the look-out.'

'Yes. And Bettine would not dream of marrying him. You know, grandmother, I think mother produces all these young men for Bettine so that she can reproach her after-wards that she is still single. She loves reproaching people. Still, she can't touch me any more. I am a married woman, thank God. Did I tell you, that Oscar bought me a white ermine cloak in Paris? Imagine. Real ermine. I shall be like a queen. Mother says it is ridiculous and that I am much too young for it. But I don't see it. Do you? After all, I have got to have something enjoyable at least.'

'Yes, dear.'

'And when I think, when I was twelve, I had that tippet of white rabbit which Aunt Louise gave me, with the little black tails like fringes on it, and Emma made such a fuss about it and said it was like real ermine. Of course, she did not know any better. You don't see ermine every day, do you?'

'Certainly not,' said the old lady.

'And if anybody had told me a year ago that I would ever have such a wonderful fur coat I would not have believed it. Life is an amazing thing, isn't it? Once at school when we had to learn about Africa and grumbled a lot, the teacher said to us: How do you know you won't be there one day? She was quite right. I don't know much yet, but after all I have seen a bit already, and I must say things turn out so surprisingly. I often want to laugh out loud when we have a dinner-party and everybody comes and is so stiff and stuck up and all the men kiss my hand and they listen when I say something and take me seriously. If they knew how Uncle Tony's groom used to hit me across the bottom and yell at me when my seat was not right and what words he used. And how mother boxed my ears when I was cheeky. No, grandmother, I will say this, that marriage has a lot of advantages.'

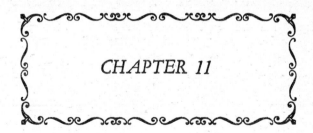

CHAPTER 11

IT WAS nearly eleven o'clock when Margot entered her own bedroom. It was by tradition a young girl's room. Alice had occupied it until her first marriage; later on Bettine, and afterwards Mr. Birk's daughter before her last illness. It was not furnished in the gimcrack, haphazard way prevalent in the castle. The late Mr. Birk-Borovec had arranged it specially for Alice, on the occasion of her seventeenth birthday and with the idea, as was only too obvious, that young womanhood is comparable to a rose.

The walls were covered with a paper patterned with rosebuds. The hangings were of linen with a design of rose-wreaths. The wardrobe was white with carved garlands of roses. The pink carpet showed roses of a deeper pink and, to enhance the picture of youth and spring, there were rugs of lambskin in front of the bed and dressing-table.

As a small yellow chest of drawers stood in one corner, Emma, with the perversity of perfect servants, always alluded to the room as the 'yellow room'.

Margot lit a candle. She sat down on the bed and began to undress slowly. There was a cough and a knock at the door.

'Come in,' she called.

Emma entered, carrying a tray. Despite the advanced time, she was still clad in the prim black and white of her calling. Only her bare head, deprived of the bonnet, indicated that the official hours of her day were over.

'Dear me,' she said and clicked her tongue. 'Eleven o'clock struck and gone and we are not in bed yet?' She placed the tray on the yellow chest and smoothed the embroidered cloth.

'Don't look so surprised, Emma,' replied Margot. 'If you had not known I was still up, you would not have come. Ah, it's so nice to see you.'

'You did not always think so, Miss Margot.'

'No, of course not. The way you used to drag me out of bed at seven every morning. And you always said, school-sausage get up. Schoolsausage. Do you remember?' She giggled.

'We have all got to go through the mill,' replied Emma. She drew a chair up to the bed and sat down; a liberty which she would not have taken with the other members of the family. 'But you have been a good girl and got up every morning and went to school and got educated and married a nice gentleman. One thing leads to another.'

'Yes it does, Emma. What have you brought me, milk?'

'A nice glass of milk. That's what you should drink while you are here. In town it's all horrible and skimmed off and blue and no goodness left in it. Even Mr. Oscar, with all his money, can't buy you a proper glass of milk like this. And some spice-biscuits. You must eat something to build yourself up. You are as thin as a spring chicken.'

'But I eat a lot, Emma. I don't know where it goes to. It's all the strain, you know. Standing in the picture galleries for hours in the heat.'

'Ah, but it was worth it. All the things you have seen. Cook has kept all the picture post cards you sent. I don't hold with it. Not that they aren't nice, because they are, but you can't go by them. A place is never as it looks on the card.' She got up and fetched Margot's dressing-gown. 'Now get undressed and put it on quickly, before you catch a cold. And then I'll brush your hair. You never liked to brush it yourself.'

'But I don't need anything on, Emma,' protested the young girl, as she slipped off her underclothes. 'It is so hot still.'

The maid stood over her with the gown. 'Hurry up, Miss Margot; it's hot, but it's treacherous. You have got the windows open and the night air is blowing in. It's not healthy; it's all the dampness from the park. Before you know where you are, you will have a pneumonia or a pleurisy.'

'Oh, nonsense, Emma.' Margot slipped into her night-dress and wrapped herself into the dressing-gown.

'Isn't it lovely?' she asked. 'The yellow silk and the black lace? I got it in Milan. Mother says only white is decent and she is shocked. But everybody wears coloured stuffs now. All the fashionable people.'

'It's beautiful,' answered Emma. 'But you want to be careful how it is washed. You can never tell if the colours are fast. And you should not make fun of illness, Miss Margot. My brother was just like you, and then he got pleurisy out

107

of the blue and he did not feel like laughing then. Now, you
don't want to get it. Every time you breathe it's like a knife
stuck between your ribs, he told me. Now come and I'll do
your hair. You want to have your hair nice and glossy when
Mr. Oscar comes.'

'It does not matter what it looks like,' said Margot as she
submitted to the brush. 'I mean it does, but he always finds
fault with it. He says it makes him feel ill when my hair is
untidy. And then he says, that if he wouldn't know it for
certain, he would not believe that I am of a good family.
Whatever I do, he always corrects me. He says he does not
know how I was brought up.'

'That's understandable,' replied Emma. She put the brush
down, picked up a comb and quickly made a parting. 'That's
nice and straight. I will brush it away from the middle now.
Your hair is lovely, Miss Margot; I should not really tell
you, because it might make you vain, but it's the truth and
not a lie. And don't let it get you down when Mr. Oscar
talks like that. It's only because he is not a Birk himself. The
Ritters never had a place in the country. The old Mr. Ritter
used to serve in his own shop, I was told. Did his own books
and stood behind the counter. I hope you don't mind me
saying so, Miss Margot, but you know it better than I do,
and, of course, I don't mind old Mr. Ritter keeping a shop –
we have all got to make our living somehow and not everybody can have a castle, but if they do, they are nearer to
kings than to others. And that is what makes Mr. Oscar fret
so much. Because he has married you and you have grown
up in it and he's had to work to be where he is. It's always
the people who are used to nothing decent at home who

make the greatest fuss in the hotels. My brother worked in hotels in Vienna and Prague and Biarritz, and he always said so. The real gentleman never complains, he said. And if Mr. Oscar pulls you up because of this or that, or when he says something to us – because he always does, you know – it's only because he wants to show that he has got everything at his finger-tips, the same as the Birks.'

'How right you are, Emma. Of course, we don't think so much about family and all that. We are what we are and it's natural to us. But it is there, at the back of our minds, just the same. I know some years ago I passed through the old town square and it was Christmas-time and there was the fair. I would have loved to buy one of those lollipops. Not the white ones. The pink ones. I always think God never meant anything to look as pink as those lollipops. But anyhow, I was only a child and I was dying for one. But then, I pulled myself together and thought: No, Margot, you can't. You can't walk through the town sucking a lollipop. You are a Birk. That was enough.'

'I quite believe it, Miss Margot. That's as it should be. And that is what Mr. Oscar has never had and it makes him sore. Why, only the other day Prince Podolsky was here and he said to your Uncle Tony that from all he's seen, there were archdukes who didn't have a place anything like Kirna.'

She put the brush down with an impressive gesture and looked triumphantly at Margot in the glass. 'And what's worse,' she added, 'so many of them have lost their castles and live in flats and rooms and heaven knows how.'

She shook her head. 'Everything is upside down since the war, and there's the Ritters – but I suppose it's all for the best.' She picked the brush up again. 'But it's a shame, just the same.'

She tidied the dressing-table and flicked the palm of her hand across its surface.

'Well, there, Miss Margot, you've got to be thankful for what you have got and that your Uncle Tony and the old lady still sit in Kirna, as their father has done and his father before them. Now off you go to bed; it's half past already. I'll tuck you in. You will have to hurry up to get through all your sleep by tomorrow morning.'

'Oh, you are sweet, Emma. The way you talk, I always feel better afterwards.'

'Dear me, we should feel good all the time.'

'I know, Emma. But things are not as they should be, like what you said about picture post cards. And I must not think any more about the family. My grandmother says that if you are proud, you must be intelligent enough to conceal it. So there. And good night.'

'Good night and God bless you, Miss Margot.' And with that Emma withdrew and closed the door so quickly, noiselessly and firmly as only well-trained servants do.

CHAPTER 12

THE NEXT day was a Saturday. It was clear and sunny as before, but the strong breeze which had risen during the night was still blowing.

A boy with a wheelbarrow was picking leaves and twigs from the turf bordering the rose-parterre, while another one swept up the remnants of two broken flower-pots from the terrace. The stone cherub raised in the centre of the fountain was mirrored in blurred outlines in the basin below, where the water was green and glistening with floating leaves. Strips of white cobwebs and the feathery seeds of dandelions sailed through the air. Beyond the terraced lawn, where the grass grew long and thick, the tall marguerites were swaying up and down like white foam cresting emerald waves.

Mrs. Birk-Borovec had installed herself with her needlework in the shelter of the garden-room. Above her head a few loose strands of ivy were beating against the stone arches and their shadows flew like dark garlands among the painted birds on the wall.

Alice was seated by her side with an open account book.

Each time her finger moved past a group of figures, she tapped her foot on the floor. She drew her breath in and turned a page. 'Twenty crowns for salt in the last fortnight,' she said. 'Mama, it's hair-raising. Do you really think it's possible? I know what she is doing. When she wants to have a good fire in the range and is too lazy to stoke it up properly, she throws a handful of salt into the fire. I know her tricks. Sheer waste. I must talk to her again.'

She fell silent and scanned another page. 'It seems to make hardly a difference, whether we are in Prague or in Kirna,' she remarked. 'The money goes just the same. And yet here everything is for the asking. I find it most depressing. I could weep, mama, I could positively howl, I can assure you.'

'Wait till we get to the end of the month, Alice,' said the old lady. 'It will give you a better view on the spendings.'

'Very well, mother.' She closed the book with a sharp movement. 'Now, what I want to know, who is coming to Boleslav this afternoon? You, of course, and Bettine and young Marek. What about Uncle Tony? And what about Margot? Personally, I think she should go back to Prague after lunch. Somebody can take her to the station. If Uncle Tony does not come with us, he could drive her.'

'I am sure that she won't go yet,' replied the old lady. 'And why should she leave? She will enjoy the excursion.'

'You are always giving in to her, mama. She got Oscar's letter this morning and she should be on her way. And to-morrow is Sunday and the boys will be here and she will go less than ever. She is absolutely heartless. All out for her pleasure. When she arrived yesterday, what did she talk about? The new stationmaster. Not a word about Oscar and not caring either. The new stationmaster. That's Margot all over.'

She played with the book on her lap. The old lady continued with her crochetwork; it was a strip of lace formed of minute squares and interspersed with trefoils.

'I think I'll go and talk to her now,' said Alice. 'After all, that's what I am here for. If Margot does not know what is right, it is up to me to tell her.'

'I should not say anything, Alice,' remarked the old lady. 'She is a bit tense, you know.'

'Is there anything wrong? Has she had a difference with Oscar? I wish you would tell me.'

'No, nothing, Alice. But she has been under a strain. Sight-seeing and travelling——'

'Nonsense, mama. You'd think she was made of sugar.'

Alice looked up. Mr. Birk had entered. He threw himself on a chair and swished with his riding-crop round his boots. 'Damn the flies. You'd think the wind would make them tired. But no fear.'

'Did you see the damage in the park, Uncle Tony?' asked Alice. 'The tree on the Fieldmarshal's Hill?'

'Have I seen it? Of course I have seen it. Do you think I am blind or what?'

'Tony,' said his sister, 'my handkerchief is on the floor.'

'Curse it!' he shouted jovially as he bent down. His chair creaked. He breathed heavily. 'Can't think why you carry a handkerchief. If I feel like it, I blow my nose in my fingers and nobody thinks the worse of me for it '

'You are disgusting, Uncle Tony.'

'Tony, we have just been talking about this afternoon. Are you coming with us to Boleslav?'

'I am if I am invited. If not, I'll stay at home and imagine it, hahaha.'

'That settles it, then,' said Alice. She rose and tucked the book under her arm. She tugged at her dress. 'I will go and see Margot now. Do you know where she is, Uncle Tony? She showed Marek round the greenhouses, didn't she?'

'That was an hour ago, Alice. You'd better sit down on your bottom again; you won't get her now.'

'What do you mean?'

'She is trotting with Prince Podolsky round the coachhouses. On the blasted carthorses, too; at least, that's how I left them. I suppose they are in the agent's parlour now, drinking coffee.'

'I'm – I am speechless. Carthorses? And Prince Podolsky?'

'Hang it all, Alice. You know Prince Podolsky and you know the horses.'

'Can you explain, please?'

'What do you want me to explain? He has come over to have a look at my Lipizianers. And he is still looking at them. And he has always had a weakness for Margot. So he is combining the two, haha.'

Alice gave him a fierce look.

'There is nothing in it. It is all proper and above board. And now they are with the agent's wife. That's respectable enough. What more do you want?'

'I feel ashamed. And amazed. And why, if the Prince is here, have you not brought him over? He could have had his coffee with us.'

'You'll never understand, Alice, if you grow to be a hundred years old. For one thing, he's come to see my horses and not you. And then, why should I invite him here? I know what's done as well as anybody. He is Prince Podolsky and I am Tony Birk and he's come on business and that's all there is to it. When you go to buy a pound of sugar at your grocer's you don't stay to tea with them either. We are what we are; we've not been picked up in the gutter, but there is still a difference between him and us. And I'm the first to respect it. I'll be damned if I throw myself on to anybody.'

'I still don't see it, Uncle Tony. We are not good enough for him – very well. But the agent?'

'That's different again, damn it. The agent is so much out of it that it makes it possible again. But we can't, Alice. Just because we are so near his own set-up. That's where it gets dangerous.'

Alice resumed her seat and tapped with her foot on the floor.

'And Margot?'

'Ah well, a pretty girl is a pretty girl all the world over, Alice, so what?'

'It's most improper, to say the least of it. And so useless; she is a married woman, so there is no sense in it any more. And if she was not married, he would not think of marrying her either; because she is not his class. Besides, he is a married man himself. What's the good of it all, I ask you? I don't understand.'

'I do. But never mind, Alice.'

He bent down and with the thong of his crop scraped a crust of mud from his boot.

'Mind you,' he continued, 'nowadays the gentlemen of the Republic have decided that there is no aristocracy and they think that's the end of it. But you can't kill the nobility. You can twist it round and turn it upside down, but it will always exist. Only the other day – I had to laugh. I went to Kratice to see the Prince and he asked me to have a bite with them. You know how they live, in the lodge and the castle empty – and the whole thing – well, pretty miserable, they just can't make ends meet. There we sat round the table and on the table a wax-cloth and that's what we were eating off. And the Princess was a bit embarrassed and made excuses the way the table was laid and said it was proletarian. You should have seen the Prince. He got properly annoyed with her. Blast it, he said, no respectable worker would sit down at such a table. Any labourer would have a white cloth. We eat like this, the way no decent workman would. And that is the difference between the workers and us. I thought it was jolly clever of him. As I said before, you can't get them down.'

'I don't see anything clever in it,' replied Alice and gave him another fierce glance. 'He can't help being poor, but he needn't shout it from the rooftops. Still, that's neither here nor there. I am worried.'

'Don't worry so much, Alice,' said the old lady. 'Let Margot have her fun. Why shouldn't she?'

'Because it's not right. You always give in to her. She should be more conscious of her position. Do you think I ever rode round on carthorses?'

'Of course you didn't, Alice. Because you never had the guts, hahaha. You were glad enough to cling on what they call a lady's horse. Never mind. Forgiven and forgotten.'

CHAPTER 13

In the early afternoon the breeze died down and the sun shone golden in the blue sky.

Up to then there had been the heat of late August, fiery and drowsy at the same time, the heat which blunts the outlines on the horizon with a mist and blurs the near surroundings with a coating of dust and dulls under waves of shimmering air the bright fruit in the green leaves and the red and blue flowers amidst the wheat.

Now the air was clear and the sunlight hard. It showed up the places where the green copper squares on the turret above the stables had been patched. It showed that the gilded weather-vane was tarnished and the white paling on both sides of the stone poodles was dirty and peeling.

The open victoria had been rolled out of the coach-house. This big shell, built for comfort and pleasure, stood on the cobbles like on a deserted beach. The light wood was burnished and glossy like burnt sugar and the seats of blue velvet, quilted and buttoned, looked black in the strong light.

Prochazka came out of the harness room. He was in shirt-sleeves and his hat was pushed out of his forehead. He beat his arms up and down. 'Shoo – shoo,' he called, trying to look fierce. A swarm of pigeons and starlings fluttered reluctantly up in the air and settled down again. He walked up to the carriage and slowly circled round it. Sometimes he stopped and stroked the varnished wood.

It was twenty minutes later when Mrs. Birk-Borovec made an appearance in the courtyard. She wore grey foulard with a strip of white-embroidered cherries across her breast. Her hair stood in a high and wide curve above the square forehead. Her double chin fell majestically over the band of grey satin round her throat.

Behind her – at a respectful distance of three paces – stepped Emma, carrying the old lady's parasol. It was of straw-coloured silk, trimmed with three rows of frilled lace and the ivory handle was carved in the shape of an owl.

'Look at her, at that Emma, that creature,' said Alice to Bettine, as they crossed the gravel space. 'There she is, carrying the parasol and making a pretty snout, all to get into mama's good books. As though mama couldn't carry it herself. I often say, many a young woman would envy her her strength. But no. Emma's got to waste time. I can think of all sorts of jobs which she could do in the house. I could weep when I look at her; I could positively howl, I assure you.'

For a while they walked in silence, each lady holding the brim of her large straw hat. Alice's was white and stiff with a prim black ribbon. Bettine's was of undulating Florentine straw and decorated with a sprawling wreath of field flowers.

'Look behind you, Bettine,' said Alice. 'Are they coming?'

'Yes, they have just come out. Margot and Marek and Uncle Tony.'

'Good. I wanted to tell you.' Alice gripped her hat more tightly and lowered her voice. 'I had a talk with Margot. About going back to Prague. Mama advised me against it, but I always feel if you are reasonable and understanding people will be reasonable with you. I had no trouble with Margot at all. She immediately agreed when I broached the subject. She is going back tomorrow after breakfast. She will take the ten-thirteen.'

'What a pity she is leaving,' remarked Bettine and for the first time turned her head and looked at her sister. 'She's hardly arrived. I don't know why Oscar insists. You'd think he could spare her for a day or two. Such love. I don't like it.'

'I am sorry to say, Bettine, there are things which you don't understand. Once you are married yourself, then you can talk. I am not a woman of many words, but even if I were – I could not explain.'

'I don't see what there is to explain,' replied Bettine. 'He is selfish and inconsiderate. Anybody can see that, without being married.' She lowered her head.

Alice hastened her steps. 'If you don't mind,' she said, 'I beg to disagree. And Margot saw my point straight away. Not that I had any doubts about it. And please, Bettine, if you want to do me a favour, keep your shoulders back. There is a proper way of doing everything, even riding in a carriage, and if you could see yourself, with your slouched-up back. Now let's go and talk to mama, shall we? She is sitting there all alone.'

It was decided that Alice and Bettine were to sit on the main seat with the old lady; Margot and Raoul Marek on the narrow bench facing them; and Mr. Birk on the box with Prochazka.

'I hope this little trip won't bore you, Mr. Marek,' remarked Alice. 'We do things very simply nowadays. In the old days, before the war, we used to drive out in a different style. A footman on the box with Prochazka and one behind, standing on the little stepping-board at the back of the coach. And with his arms crossed all the time, Mr. Marek, in the proper way. Mind you, we used to tease Uncle Tony about it; it was his idea. We used to call him Lord Birk, Earl of Kirna. We have very simple tastes really; we don't pretend to be *grands seigneurs*, and I always said, just one footman, yes – that's what people expect from us, but two – it's not really necessary, is it?'

Margot looked radiant and smiling. No, she did not want a hat against the sun; she did not mind, she was not as old as that yet. 'I am sorry, mother, I did not mean it. I really didn't. I don't know what I meant.'

'I don't mind this sort of remark, Margot,' replied Alice, who was more indulgent than usual, probably because of the slightly festive air due to their outing. 'I always like to see clearly in all matters and nobody can say that I ever attempt to deceive myself. I am not as young as I was – I can't deny it. Although it's not so very long ago that people thought you were my sister. But I remember when I was young and pretty I took better care of my skin.'

'You mean when you were young, Alice,' shouted Mr. Birk.

'How wonderful!' exclaimed Margot. 'Uncle Tony still makes the same jokes. Grandmother, how long has he nursed this one?'

'Ever since your mother went to her first ball,' said the old lady. 'But even then it was not new. He used to try it on with your Aunt Louise before that. This and the question about the dinner see him through every family gathering.'

'All set?' roared Mr. Birk. He turned round on his seat and balanced his hat on his riding-stick above his head. It was a shabby dark green felt and the chamois beard stuck into the ribbon had a desperate likeness to a shaving-brush.

Emma stuck her head into the carriage. 'I have put the silver mug underneath the back seat, madam, because you'll want to drink.'

'Very well, Emma,' said the old lady.

'No, mama, it will only roll about and be a nuisance,' protested Alice.

'What are we going to drink?' asked Raoul Marek. 'Are they taking their own table service with them?' he thought. 'It would be a bit thick. Footmen, yes – but that!'

'It's because we are going to the Cuckoo Mill,' Margot informed him. She shrugged and cried: 'I say, put it inside the box; there it will be out of the way.'

'No, that's no good,' said Bettine. 'It will knock against the brake-stone. He always keeps a brake-stone there.'

'Then we must wrap it up, mama.'

'This will do,' said the old lady. 'We'll keep the mug where it is. Bettine, will you please open my sunshade? The spring is a bit stiff.'

The horses pulled and stepped out. Emma fell back and curtseyed.

'Good-bye, Emma, good-bye,' shouted Margot. She leaned over the young man's shoulder and waved her handkerchief. He watched her with growing irritation. 'She is completely unselfconscious,' he thought bitterly. 'It never occurs to her that she is touching a man.'

'Sit back, Margot,' said Alice. 'For one thing one does not shout. Do you ever hear me shout? Even Bettine – does she ever shout?'

'Can you find my second glove, Alice?' said the old lady.

'Yes, mama, here. I was sitting on it. And secondly, what do you want to say good-bye for? You see her the whole day long.'

'I say, Miss Bettine,' ventured Raoul Marek. 'We are going to the Cuckoo Mill. Is it an inn? In Boleslav?'

'No, it's on the way. And we always stop there.'

'There is a spring. One has to drink the water. Because there's iron in it,' said Margot. 'You've got to swallow it quickly, because it's bad for your teeth, but you've got to drink it because it's good for you. We always do.'

'And another thing,' continued the young man. 'I hope you won't mind if I ask – but everything is so strange – I mean so fascinating – all the names and customs. I was thinking of what Mrs. Birk-Borovec was saying, about the joke with the dinner.'

'Oh, that!' said Bettine. 'Really, it's so silly, it's hardly worth telling. It is one of Uncle Tony's tricks of making people embarrassed. If he is invited somewhere to a big dinner, he sits down and eats and eats, and when they are about to leave the table, he shouts very loud, so that all can hear it – I say, madam, and what are we going to have for dinner?'

'And the marvellous thing is,' added Margot, 'that Aunt Mila in Semtin – Uncle Max's wife – rises every time, you know. It makes her furious.'

They rolled at a leisurely pace along the highway, followed by a cloud of dust. On either side, behind the ditches and the plum trees, one field followed another, sometimes broken by a strip of cultivated poppies which with their high and swaying stalks and their waxy white and slightly rosy petals looked unspeakably lovely amidst the sturdy green of sugar beet and the placid yellow of wheat.

After a quarter of an hour's driving, the River Elbe appeared on their right, and alongside its sluggish and muddy waters the fields gave way to marshy grass, clumps of willows, masses of sedge and tall bushes of white flowering bindweed. The young man looked at the countryside and felt its sullen charm, and it occurred to him for the first time in his life that this was the land that had brought forth the Bohemian folk-songs with their slowly flowing tunes, their darkly veiled lamentations, and their sad surrender to daily life.

They encountered a group of peasants dressed in the black, stiff Sunday clothes of country people. The young women wore fashionable hats, the older ones fringed and tasselled shawls knotted beneath the chin. As the carriage approached, they lined up against the ditch. The men doffed their caps, the women curtseyed.

'Here we go, folks, and may God bless you,' shouted Mr.

Birk and balanced his hat on his stick with great good humour. The ladies nodded.

'You do know an awful lot of people, Mrs. Birk-Borovec,' remarked the young man.

'Not at all, Mr. Marek. They know me, but I don't know them.'

'Well said, Ida,' exclaimed her brother. He turned round on his seat and surveyed them cheerfully. 'We are as well known here as a bad penny, there's no getting away from it. In the old days when the Emperor used to come to Brandys to pay a visit to the Dragoons, when he met my mother, he always greeted her first, before she had time to curtsey. Mind you, I always envied him this one privilege he had. Not that I would want to be Emperor, Heaven forbid, but just this one little thing of Court etiquette. You don't remember it, you young tripehound – that was well before your time; but when I think of it, it still makes my ears turn hot.'

'Tony, please,' said the old lady and held up her hand clad in a pale grey kid glove. 'Spare us your feelings.'

'That's the way they treat me, young Raoul. All my life I have been shushed and shut up. I am used to it. But just think, as I was saying. There he would stand, our Emperor Franz-Joseph, at balls and receptions, you know. And the ladies would come up in front of him, one after the other, like geese walking in a row. They would sink down, deep down; it was not easy to curtsey – they had to practise it for weeks. And you know what Court dress was like. All bare shoulders and a good bit beyond that, if you get me. This was all laid down in the rules to an inch. So that standing where he did, the Emperor our Lord, he had a damn good view of all there was to see, you can take my word for it. Not bad, eh? The finest view in the Monarchy, I always think.'

'It is a pity it's all gone,' ventured the young man. 'I just mean speaking in general. I don't remember much. But the Emperor's birthday. Or when he went up the river in Prague with the fanfares sounding.'

'Yes, yes,' said Alice. 'Ta-tee-ta-ta, that's how it always went. And we all wore white dresses.'

'And the people,' said the old lady, 'when they heard the tune, always hummed ta-tee-ta-ta, there goes our money. There is something to be said for their point of view, too, I think.'

'Well, I don't know,' said Alice. 'It was nice, just the same.'

'Of course it was,' exclaimed Mr. Birk. 'The Emperor's birthday, that was something. And what have we got now? Do you hear that the President ever has a birthday? Of course he hasn't. He would not dare.'

For a minute he fell into a reverie. His chin rested on his fist, his elbow on his knee. His bristly white hair glinted in the sun. With his red hanging cheeks and his wrinkled short nose he looked harmless and old. But the string-coloured gaberdine suit, stretched tightly over arms and thighs, revealed powerful muscles and his body seemed to have an alertness of its own.

'Although I don't know,' he added. 'Must not judge people. You can't put the clock back and the President looks decent enough. Gets up at six every morning and has a ride. Not a bad fellow. On a white horse, too, hahaha.'

'Let it be, Tony,' said the old lady and she pointed with her parasol at the coachman's back. 'We are about to take the turning to the left, Mr. Marek. This will lead us to the mill.'

'Oh yes?'

The mill lay in the heart of a small wood. It was a low derelict building which had once been painted white. It was surrounded by heaps of rubble, wooden planks and stones, partly overgrown by lush green weeds. Most of the windows were bereft of glass and their edges covered with cobwebs and creeper; they lent the house an appearance of brooding blindness, like the stare of empty eye sockets in a skull.

'It's terribly romantic,' cried Margot as she clambered out of the carriage. 'The ruins in Rome are nothing in creepiness compared to this. I think there are rats. But they don't show themselves.'

'You might keep your speculations to yourself,' said Alice.

'Well, if it was all clean and tidy, it would not be so lovely, mother. Oscar is always so keen on everything being hygienic, but I think dirt is more interesting.'

'This mill was given to a local young lady,' said Mr. Birk to Raoul Marek. 'By the Emperor, so they say. For services rendered. I can't vouch for it, but quite possible, you know.'

'I don't know what's the matter with you, Uncle Tony,' remarked Alice. 'The way you keep harping about the Emperor today, and you put him in such a queer light.'

'I am getting historically minded, Alice. Getting warmed up. Going to Boleslav puts you into that mood. And for me, that's what history is. The rest can go to hell.'

'This is not a hunting party, Uncle Tony, this is a family excursion.'

'All the same to me, Alice.'

They picked their way through the undergrowth among stones and mossy ground, towards the mill-pond. Duckweed had spread its glaucous network over the surface and only here and there a patch of water could be seen, dull in the brownish-green twilight beneath the tangle of fir branches.

A few steps away from the bank stood a smooth and rounded chunk of wood. From an opening in the middle issued a thin trickle of water, splashing on the ground and running in a groove which meandered into the wood till it was lost to the view.

'That's it,' said Margot. 'You see how yellow it is? That's the iron. It's awfully healthy.'

She returned to the carriage to fetch the mug.

'I might have thought of it,' she murmured and tapped her forehead.

'What one has not got in the head, one has to have in the legs,' remarked Alice darkly and gave her a reproachful glance.

They all drank in silence. First the old lady, then her two daughters, then Mr. Birk, Margot, and finally the young man. The water was so cold that it took his breath away; it left a bitter taste in the mouth.

'I am glad Oscar isn't here,' said Margot with a grimace. 'He would not approve at all. Everybody drinking out of the same cup.'

She wiped her lips with the back of her hand, taking care that her mother should not see her. Finally she dried the mug with a handful of moss and grass.

'It's a pity I can't paint,' she mused. 'I should love to

have a picture of the mill. Every time I would look at it, I would feel a cold shiver down my spine. Wouldn't it be lovely?'

Nobody answered. The old lady glanced at her sideways.

'Now come on, gee up, the whole lot of you!' cried Mr. Birk. 'You are beauties. Standing about like sheep when it thunders.'

They returned to the victoria and got seated. Prochazka rubbed his eyes furtively and adjusted his hat. He cracked the whip halfheartedly. The horses stepped out and the carriage gave a jolt which brought a stifled scream from Bettine and a 'Really, this is disgraceful' from Alice.

'I love this sort of thing,' said Margot. 'There is nothing nicer than a big bump in the road, so that you think you will fly out. Or when I'm on a horse and it shies and rears right up in the air and you think you are done for. Uncle Tony is marvellous in that way. He can make the horses buck so that you think you are in mortal danger and it makes you feel good. There's nothing he can't do with a horse.'

'I always said you should have become a circus rider,' said Mr. Birk.

'Yes, that would be the life for me, Uncle Tony. Every night in the ring in red velvet and spangles and a rose behind my ear. And the limelight on me and everybody watching and afterwards bouquets of flowers and love letters.'

'If that's what you are after, you can have it without the bother of performing on a horse, hang it all. Although, I suppose you are a bit on a tight rein now, haha. Back to stables tomorrow, eh?'

'Uncle Tony,' exclaimed Alice, 'I wish you wouldn't——'

'What have I said now that's wrong? Am I to talk about the weather and the crops the whole time? They don't take any notice of me, in any case. The way you ladies carry on, it sometimes makes me wonder how you ever manage – children and all that. Only this morning the Prince said to me he doesn't know where Margot gets her temperament from. Not from Alice, I said, no fear. She's got it from me, of course. And from Ida. What do you say, Ida, eh?'

The old lady smiled. 'You put me in a difficult position, Tony.'

'We are getting near the town, Mr. Marek,' said Bettine. 'This is the Crown Inn. They have very good food there. The best thing to do is to visit it in spring and order young roast goose with new potatoes and cucumber salad. The proprietress is very fat; she is a sort of landmark in the district. When she serves the meal, she always says – it's young and it's tender and it's good. It has become a standing joke. Because she is so used to saying it that she even says it when she pours out the coffee.'

They passed the inn and a string of small modern houses; then a row of neglected-looking buildings, a school, the police station, the post office. The highway changed into a badly paved and narrow street with children playing in front of shuttered shops and groups of old men with long pipes standing on street corners.

A square opened in front of them and they had to stop for a while to make way for a motor car.

They drove up to the town hall and halted in front of the arcades above which the early baroque façade rose with grace and dignity. Its outline was scrolled and narrowed towards the top. On each corner, level with the first floor, was a pillared niche with a saint's figure in blue, gold and red. The three central windows were surmounted by carved stone architraves.

The church of St. Wenceslas stood on the opposite corner. It looked small and modest under the steep and tumble-down slate roof. Yet it was neatly whitewashed and the arched window, the domed portico and the curved bay fell into the pattern of ease and elegance beloved by the baroque. The belfry was fat and squat, as is the custom in this part of Bohemia, where the steeples do not point skywards and where the peasants only raise their eyes to the stars in order to predict the weather.

'It's no good standing in front of the Mayor's kennel,' announced Mr. Birk. 'Inside there's nothing to see and out-side – once you've seen it, you've seen it. So off to the church. I hope young Raoul feels duly awestricken; we are standing on historical ground, you, I, the whole lot of us, whether we like it or not.'

'Don't you think we should find the verger, Tony?' asked the old lady. 'He does not like to be done out of his *pour-boire.*'

'Very well, Ida. I think he's gone to ground, but I'll see what I can do.'

They went to the side entrance, which lay in the shade of old chestnut trees. Two hens were picking over the grass. The door, much more ancient than any other part of the building, was of black-brown wood, pitted and grooved by the ravages of time. It was bordered by stout iron nails and a gleaming brass ring was attached to the latch.

'This is the ring,' said the old lady, 'which Saint Wenceslas gripped when he was murdered by his brother.'

'Is this it – is it really?' asked Raoul Marek.

'They keep the ring in remarkably good shape, I always think,' said Bettine.

'The door looks very old, though – I mean, very convincing,' ventured the young man. 'But surely the church – it does not make sense.'

'Of course it doesn't,' shouted Mr. Birk. 'But we've got an answer to every question, haven't we, Ida? We did not wait for young flipperty-gibbets like you to come and pick holes into good King Wenceslas. You pettifoggers, you are all the same.'

'What is the answer, then, Mr. Birk?'

'The old church got burnt down, of course. Churches always do, you know. And they built this one round the door, so to speak. Now I leave you to the care of the ladies. And no blaspheming; the hens don't like it.'

'It's staggering when you come upon something which really happened,' said the young man. 'I must confess I always thought it was merely a legend.'

'It is a very interesting story,' said the old lady. 'Not the happening in itself, but the issues behind it. The King, a converted Christian, goes to Mass every morning. His brother Boleslav, the leader of the pagan Bohemian tribes, goes after him with a dagger and chases him right up to the church. The King, not very martyrlike, tries to make a dash for it, because once inside he is safe. But he only gets as far as the door, this door. In those days, in my opinion, it was merely a struggle for power. Later on the King was canonized and became a Christian martyr. Very pretty, I'm sure, the good Christian against the wicked heathen. That was how we learnt it at school. But now, Mr. Marek, they have turned it the other way round. I always felt that the King was a questionable figure. But then, who isn't in history? The traitor of today becomes the liberator of a nation tomorrow. It's a question of perspective, don't you think?'

'Oh, quite, quite, absolutely.'

'And there you are, Mr. Marek. They make the best of it nowadays. Trust the schoolteachers for that. I have always said that our schoolmarms were responsible for the break-up of the Monarchy. Once women get hold of something, they are so fanatical, you know.' She glanced at him sideways.

'There is the verger,' cried Margot.

'Now what are you going to do?' said Alice. 'You have not got a hat. I told you you should take one.'

'I will wear a handkerchief, mother. Grandmother has not got a hat either, so it's all right.'

'This is no excuse. I wash my hands of it.'

'Mrs. Birk, please, before we go in. What is the new story they dish up now.'

The old lady closed her parasol and drew with the point a circle round her feet. 'Saint Wenceslas was on the German side. That was why he became converted. It was from Germany, if you remember, that Christianity came. So he really was an enemy of the people. Boleslav remained Bohemian, independent and nationalistic, as we would say – and by stabbing his brother he committed a good deed, that is, from the new point of view.'

'Here are the keys with the man behind them,' shouted Mr. Birk, as he approached. The verger was a small old man, black-robed, and with a blue and purple mottled face.

'I announce respectfully to have wished a good afternoon,' he said, drew himself to a rigid military position and pressed his bunch of keys to his side.

'Good afternoon,' replied the others.

'Now, Kucera, how's things?' asked Mr. Birk. He took out his case and handed the man two cigarettes.

The verger waved his hand and selected a key.

'What is the news, Kucera,' asked Margot. 'I haven't seen you for ages.'

'Nothing much, miss, I mean madam. I got married last week.'

There was a general outcry.

'Did you really? What is your wife like?'

'Margot, please——' interrupted Alice.

He continued to wave his hand. 'Can't say, miss. Depends what your taste is like. Personally, I don't think she is up to much.'

Margot hid her mouth with a handkerchief and, shaking with laughter, stepped behind her grandmother.

Bettine and Raoul Marek struggled for a while, red-faced and with tears in their eyes, till they burst out laughing simultaneously.

'It's so funny,' gasped the young man. 'I mean, the way the hens scratch in the grass – I mean, right in front of the church – oh, oh.'

'Yes, the hens,' affirmed Bettine, breathless and grateful for having found an excuse. She wiped her face.

133

'We have come to see the church, Mr. Kucera,' said Alice in a loud and firm voice, and cast angry glances at Bettine.

The old lady took a silk square out of her bag and spread it over her hair. 'Shall we go, Alice, Bettine? Are you ready, Mr. Marek?'

The verger laid a hand on the door and pushed it open.

'Oh, oh,' gasped the young man, 'I thought it was locked. It looked that way. It gave me quite a start.'

'It's always open on Saturday afternoon, sir. But I got the keys out just the same. We've got to have some discipline and order. It all goes according to the drill.'

He stood aside while they advanced into the cool, dark brown interior.

The old lady went straight ahead, while Alice and Margot, the latter with a crumpled handkerchief hanging over her right ear, dipped their fingers into the basin with holy water and made a hasty genuflection, while they crossed themselves. There was a smell of incense and poor people's clothes and an air of joyless devotion. Only the pulpit, supported by a relief carving of cherubs and foliage, held a gleam of that florid and gilded and flamboyant radiance which Italian builders poured over the churches of Prague at a time when the masters of Castle Kirna spoke bad French instead of their mother tongue and when the cages in the park were alive with monkeys and exotic birds.

'If you please, madam,' said the verger to Alice. 'I announce respectfully that we have got a new holy relic from Rome.'

From past experience he knew that it was safest to address this handsome and embittered lady, because her answers never fell short of the expected and appropriate.

'That's splendid, Mr. Kucera. This is the proof of what I told you in the beginning, when Father Valerian came. He is keen, I said, you will see.'

'He is keen because he is young, Alice. That's all there is to it,' shouted Mr. Birk. 'Now come here, Kucera; I want to present you to our young friend from Prague. This is Mr. Marek, Kucera. He's a relic, too, a regular old-timer, aren't you, Kucera? And more to my liking, let me tell you. He has been in the Bosnian campaign, young Marek, first corporal and then sergeant, put that in your pipe and smoke it. There are not many about nowadays who can tell the tale. Yes, just look at him. A bit loose in the knees, perhaps, but otherwise as fit as a fiddle.'

The verger straightened his shoulders and listened with a wooden face.

'I think we had better see the relic, Tony,' said the old lady, who up to now had been reading the names of fallen soldiers inscribed on a plaque. 'Don't you think so, Mr. Kucera?' She folded her golden lorgnon.

'It's difficult to say, madam. I don't know what your taste is like. Some people like it and some don't.'

'Go along, Ida. I am going to have a chat first.'

'It's in the chancel, madam, under glass, on blue velvet. A fragment of the bones of Saint Theresa.'

As soon as the old lady was gone, the verger relaxed from his military attitude.

'Now tell me how you are getting on,' asked Mr. Birk. 'What's your new boss like, that Father Valerian?'

'He does not make any difference, sir. I just carry on and

take no notice. I don't let things like that interfere with me. The priests come and go, and when you watch them you've got to have some faith of your own, sir, or you get dizzy like. I believe in reincarnation. In my next life I'll be a moth in the preacher's wardrobe.'

'Glad to hear it, Kucera. It only shows what I have always said. In the Army they teach you sense and you can toddle about in this place for a hundred years and they'll never make an old woman of you.'

'And then, sir, when you've been about, like I have. In the Herzegovina, where they are Turkish and heathens; they are filthy dirty some of them, but they can't all be wrong, can they? And they don't bother us with missionaries up here, to turn us into Mohammedans, do they?'

'Right you are again, Kucera.'

'You'll be interested to hear, sir, that Father Adrian came to see us last week. You remember him, sir, when he was regimental chaplain in Brandys. He did not look well, sir, all drawn and thin. He's gone back to the monastery, sir, and he says to me: Kucera, he says, I'm back, he says, and we've got a new abbot. And Kucera, he says, what d'you think has become of us? We've gone pious, he says, we've got faith again, Kucera, he says, that's what's become of us, he says.'

'Can't say I am surprised,' replied Mr. Birk. 'Nothing is as it used to be. What do you expect?' He rubbed his breeches thoughtfully. 'And the new land reform act they've got out now is wicked. Still, never mind, it's no good blubbering. At least we have known what it used to be like.'

With that he went to the grille in front of the high altar to rejoin the ladies and Raoul Marek.

'We thought you'd never come, Uncle Tony,' said Alice.

'We only had a little exchange of opinions, Alice. All very proper. Now what am I to look at? These chicken bones? That's Saint Katherine, isn't it?'

'Saint Theresa, Tony,' said the old lady. 'And you said that about chicken bones already last time, when it was a different saint.'

'Can't help it, Ida. It's not my fault. If they always look like chicken bones, I say so. It's their business.'

'I propose that we go,' said Mrs. Birk-Borovec. 'I dare say we are keeping Mr. Kucera too long. We cannot impose on him any more.'

She stopped in the doorway, where the light trickling through the chestnut leaves traced a pattern resembling mediaeval wrought iron work.

She handed him some money. 'Thank you for showing us round, Mr. Kucera.' She nodded and opened her parasol.

Mr. Birk patted the verger on the shoulder and silently slipped a few coins into his pocket. Raoul Marek did the same.

In the end, Alice held out a note between pointed fingers. 'Half for you, Mr. Kucera, and the rest in the poor-box. And my compliments to the Father.'

The old man, with his heels drawn together, gave several military salutes. 'I announce respectfully that it has been a pleasure, madam – a pleasure, sir – a pleasure, madam. . . .'

CHAPTER 14

ON SUNDAY morning at half past seven the little maid knocked at Margot's bedroom door. There came a faint 'Come in.'

'Good morning, Ruzena, I am quite awake already. I wonder – will you draw the curtains?'

Margot raised herself on one elbow and then sank back again. 'I can't do it,' she murmured. 'It's no good.'

After she had wrenched the curtains apart, the maid placed a pair of yellow brocade slippers on the rug by the bed.

'I'm getting down your suitcases, miss. How many do you want, I am to ask you. I am going to do the packing while you are at breakfast. Will you be taking all your clothes back with you?'

'I really don't know, Ruzena. I am afraid – I don't feel very well. Will you send me Emma.'

The girl listened with wide-open eyes and crossed herself. 'What a pity, miss, and it's such a lovely morning – the birds are singing.'

'Don't they always?' and Margot buried her head deeper

in the pillows and averted her eyes.

'It's when you went to Boleslav yesterday, somebody must have looked at you as had the evil eye.'

'Please fetch Emma,' said Margot. She remained motionless and with lowered eyelids.

It seemed a long time before there was a cough and a knock at the door. Emma, wearing the starched blue linen dress and the white apron which was her usual morning garb, came in with her small, resolute and soundless steps.

'What is it I hear, Miss Margot? Not well? Let me have a look at you. Ah, we look quite well, not pale and not red. I suppose it's just like in the old days, that you want to get up and can't make up your mind and you want me to make it up for you.'

She approached the bed, straightened the rose-embroidered cover on the bedside table and moved the travelling clock in its maroon leather case into a better position, while she kept her eyes on the young girl.

'I wish it was as you say, Emma,' replied Margot with a wan smile. 'I suppose I don't look ill; I have not looked at myself in the glass, because I just can't manage it – but then, I don't feel ill all over, if you know what I mean, it's just that I have pains when I try to sit up or raise myself.'

'Dear me, and so all of a sudden, and yesterday you were still so gay at dinner and last thing at night. If you could make the effort and straighten up, you may be all right again, because that's what you want to be, if you are going back to Prague, and you don't want Mr. Oscar to be upset.'

'That is quite true, Emma, and of course I'll be all right, I am sure. As you say, I only should straighten up.'

She raised herself on both elbows and then pressed her lips together and let herself fall back.

'I can't do it, Emma,' she said with an embarrassed smile. 'When I lie flat I don't feel anything – at least, not most of the time – but when I sit up it hurts me across the chest and the back.'

'Dear me, what are we going to do? And only the day before yesterday I was telling you about my brother and how he was taken ill all of a sudden, just like you now, and Miss Margot was laughing about it. And what did I say? Not that it need be anything serious, heaven forbid, and you don't look feverish to me and that's something to be thankful for. But going back to town is out of the question, for today at least; I can see that. Now, don't you worry. We will send a boy to Semtin; they've got a phone there, and we'll send a word to Mr. Oscar; something tactful, because it won't be anything, I'm sure. And I'd better go now and tell madam your mother. And you will be wanting to have breakfast. What shall it be?' She went over to the window and arranged the curtains into even folds.

'Oh, nothing much, Emma. Just coffee. Or no, I think I'd rather have tea; it is lighter. And nothing else. Just tea.'

'Dear me, are we off our food?'

'Yes, I have no appetite.' Margot drew a deep breath and looked up to the ceiling with an expression of relief and embarrassment.

CHAPTER 15

'WE MUST send for the doctor, mama,' said Alice.

She stood in the old lady's bedroom with both hands laid on the brass rail of the bed. Her ash blonde hair was beautifully dressed and her face smoothly cream and pink under the careful make-up. Beneath her austere dark blue dressing-gown, a white silk blouse was visible, still unfastened in front. Her mother, sitting upright in bed and with a coffee-tray in front of her, broke the point off a croissant and spread it thickly with butter and jam.

'Have you talked to Margot?' she asked. She took a gulp of coffee.

'Of course I have talked to her, mama. She looks all right; perfectly healthy, perhaps a bit pale. But then, I used to be pale, too, when I was her age. . . . She'll grow out of it. She paused and looked down on the floor. 'This rug is disgraceful, mama. You must get a new one. There are some modern ones in the shops now, with new designs.'

'I don't like them,' said the old lady.

'Neither do I,' replied Alice.

'Are you sure you want to send for the doctor?' asked the

old lady. 'You can never tell. It may be an indisposition and pass off in a day. Besides, it's Sunday.'

'Oh, ridiculous, mama. As though he would mind. No, what I feel is this. If it was anybody else, I would say you are right, mama, and wait and see. But Margot should go back to Prague. And besides, it is not really so much for her own sake that I am anxious. After all, we all go through this and that in life and not always very pleasant; I don't have to tell you this, mama, and we have to get on with it just the same. The thing is, that it is everybody's duty to be as well as they can be, for the sake of the others. And that's why I absolutely insist. If people can be well, then they must see to it that they are. That is the way I look at it.'

For a while there was silence in the room except for the ticking of a clock and the crunching and swallowing sounds as Mrs. Birk-Borovec completed her breakfast. In the end, she frankly smacked her lips with the dignity of an old peasant and dabbed her mouth with a small napkin. Then she leaned back against the pillows and straightened the plait of white hair which hung like a heavy rope over one shoulder.

'If you would be good enough, Alice, to take my tray – yes, on the washstand will do. I dare say you must have it your way. Margot is your daughter, not mine.'

'But do you agree, mama?'

'I understand, Alice. You always make yourself very clear – which is an advantage. We all must be well, whether we like it or not, in other words. Very excellent, I'm sure. But what if we don't like it? What if we prefer to be ill?'

'You are joking, mama. What on earth are you driving at?'

She dug the point of her shoe into a hole in the rug at her feet. It was an old Persian rug of that rare brownish blue colour which recalls to the mind dried moss and crushed violets.

'I am not driving at anything in particular, Alice. My mind sometimes wanders. Do unto others and so on. Very nice again, but what if the others have a different taste from yours? I don't remember who said it. I must ask Bettine; she will know. Now, I don't want to waste your time any longer.'

After Alice had left, the old lady looked for a long time at the window, where the morning sky, fresh and immaculately blue, was framed between the end of a frayed and yellowed blind and the dotted muslin, looped back with green ribbon.

CHAPTER 16

'IT IS difficult to say, doctor, because the pain comes and goes. And then, it is not always in the same place, but mainly across here, I should say. If I breathe in deeply, it hurts more, a bit like a stab in the ribs. That's why I think it must be something on the lungs.'

Margot folded her hands above the bedclothes with a pretty gesture of resignation. Her head was turned to one side. The midday sun shining through the rose-patterned hangings filled the room with a mawkish pink twilight.

Doctor Torek sat on the foot of the bed and looked at his shoes. They were broad and blunt at the top and of soft and shiny leather, countrified and urban at the same time, which was characteristic of their wearer.

He shook his head. 'There is not a sound in your lungs. They are as clear as a bell. There is nothing I can find. I should imagine that you are suffering from a muscular strain in that area. I cannot feel any stiffness there, but it may exist just the same. The patient always knows best.'

He was a tall old man with finely cut features, who still wore the side-whiskers fashionable in his younger days.

With his snowy white hair and his air of distinction, he was what people call a 'beautiful old gentleman'.

'Bedrest and bedwarmth, Margot,' he said. 'Give your body a rest. No riding and no acrobatics for a day or so. And if the pain should persist, we shall try massage and heat treatment.'

'It sounds so terribly dull, doctor.'

'Don't despise dullness, Margot. All young people do. A time will come when you will fall on your knees and pray to the Holy Virgin for a dull and uneventful life. You'll think of me yet.'

'I always think of you, doctor.'

'There, there, as flirtatious as ever. A good sign.'

She smoothed her hair and pouted. 'I don't mind staying in bed, so long as I know it's nothing to worry about.'

The doctor looked down at his shoes. 'I can completely reassure you on that. We shan't bury you yet.'

He had never considered himself to be a brilliant diagnostician, but he had been for years attached to a Cavalry Regiment, and thus there was one complaint he could tell at a glance. It was as good a case of malingering as he had ever come across.

'Well, I think that I have seen all there is to see, Margot. As far as you are concerned, that is. I shall go now and pay a visit to your grandmother. Keep warm and quiet. Eat whatever you fancy. A glass of wine or two won't hurt, and no excitements.'

With this he rose and picked up his cane and light gloves. At the door he stopped and turned round once more and raised his hand in the friendly salute which used to be the greeting of the Emperor Franz-Joseph, when receiving ovations from the people.

A few minutes later Doctor Torek was in the drawing-room, seated opposite the old lady on her French walnut settee, with a glass of plum brandy on the satinwood table by his side.

This local liqueur, as clear as water and as strong as it was clear, filled the air with a delicious aroma, fruity and sharp at once.

His cane and a pair of light gloves lay on a window-seat, together with a scattered pack of patience cards. He took a sip in silence and let his eyes stray to the window. Beyond the black-faced and golden-haired sphinxes on the settee, beyond the brown and green striped silk hangings embroidered with strings of palms and parrots, stretched the park, strange and still in the embrace of the late summer. He blinked and took another sip. 'I repeat, dear madam, no reason whatsoever to be alarmed. At the worst there is the possibility of a fibrositis, although there are indications that this is not likely. It may pass within twenty-four hours; on the other hand, it may last as long as a fortnight; in which case of course one would have to consider it as a subchronic affliction.'

'I see,' replied the old lady, with an expression which made it clear that she did not see at all, and did not want to, either.

'The whole complaint is difficult to grasp, my dear madam,' continued the doctor. 'The symptoms are – what shall I say? – slightly bizarre. This is why I don't advise any treatment at the present. I would rather watch for a further development. And then, dear madam, there is always an element of nerves which has to be considered. It is difficult to see into the mind, and when it is a case of a charming young girl, then it becomes more difficult than ever.'

'I quite agree, doctor,' replied the old lady and gave him an approving smile. She was pleased that the professional part of his visit was over.

He finished the brandy with deliberate slowness.

'Yes, the mind, the mind, dear madam. We shall never get to the bottom of it. I am greatly tempted to give you an example, although it touches a close member of your family. But then, after all these years – and I don't think you will let it go any further.'

'Help yourself to another glass, doctor.'

'Many thanks, dear madam. You recall, no doubt, your sister Louise as a young girl and as a young wife. A bit – what shall I say – lethargic? Always lying on a settee with a French novel and a box of chocolates.'

'But she had a slight temperature, if you remember, doctor,' replied the old lady.

'I know quite well. I tried to find out what made her so weak and so did my colleague Novak in Prague and that specialist – what was his name? The one who made her live on a milk diet for a year?'

'Kraus.'

'Yes, that's right. Milk diet. Result none. Injections with I don't know what any more. Nothing happened. And so on. Then Kraus had the idea that it was appendicitis. It had just become fashionable, if you remember.'

'Yes, then she was sent to Berlin, to have the operation,' said the old lady. 'There was a family row about it. Her husband said it had to be Berlin because they had better surgeons than in Prague and my brothers Tony and Gustav were furious because of the expense and said it was very easy for Karel to be generous with his wife's money. I remember that scene as though it were yesterday.'

'And I remember the repercussions, dear madam. Kraus won and we swept her off to Berlin; there was no time to lose, he said. I went there, too, in my capacity as family doctor.'

'Did you?' asked Mrs. Birk-Borovec. 'I never knew. That's interesting.'

'I did not go with her; I followed a day later. I was in the operating theatre, of course, and watched the whole performance. She made a very good recovery, if you remember, and has been a changed woman ever since. Kraus had won the day. Now if I may, not a whole, but half a glass full?'

'Help yourself, doctor. Yes, I know. She is as strong as a horse, even now. We don't speak, as you know, but sometimes I catch sight of her in the distance. She runs up the stairs like a young girl. Gets up at five every morning and does most of the housework herself, because she is too mean to pay a servant. And till late at night – so I gather – she sits and makes yarn buttons – you know, the ones on a round wire – and she sells them to a draper's shop in Prague at ten hellers a piece. I won't say what I think of it – a sister of mine – because I don't care either way. But it shows what a remarkable vitality she has. Her meanness keeps her alive, so to speak.'

'Quite so, dear madam. There is nothing like a vice to make one cling to life. I could give you examples – though

I'd better not. But to finish my story. As you know, I had been present and I assure you that there was not the slightest thing wrong with her inside. The appendix was as healthy as you could wish. Naturally, I never mentioned it. She felt revived, for which we should be grateful; she lost her fever, the faintness, she never had a day's illness since. That's why I say, dear madam, you always have to reckon with the mind.'

'I envy you your experiences, doctor,' said the old lady. 'Although no. That's not true. I don't really. I prefer not to know. At my age, one feels that nothing matters in any case. Don't you feel the same?'

'Very much so, dear madam. And what you said about experience. I've got it, of course, because I am an old man and I carry it with me whether I like it or not. They say that there is nothing like experience and that you cannot replace it by anything else. Very true, of course, but where does it get you? After all is said and done, dear madam, experience means nothing; it is a very questionable asset at the best of times. It is all so tied up with ourselves it is no more than an expression of ourselves, for all that it's worth. We can only experience that for which we are suited, dear madam, just the same as we can only be taught according to our capacity for learning. So that a fool's experiences will invariably be foolish. And here I am, just a bag full of stories and drinking all your brandy in the meantime.'

'I am very glad you came, doctor. I appreciate it very much.'

'And I am very glad to hear it, dear madam. Now I want to pay yet another visit, if you will allow me. Those *Maréchal Niel* roses down there – I could not go without a look at them. As yellow as egg yolks and with that vanilla scent. Very fascinating. What shall I say? Like a flowering custard.'

'You are most welcome to them. If you can find your way down. Or perhaps you will see Emma – she is about somewhere; and see the gardener; you know we are in his hands, as far as roses are concerned. But I don't doubt you will come to an agreement with him.'

'That excellent Emma of yours. Always with a cough before she comes into the room. Slightly hysterical, you know. There is a desire to attract attention with this cough. A very pardonable desire, I should say. Who of us does not crave attention? However . . .'

He got up and gathered his gloves and stick. 'I must be on my way. You will laugh at me, when I tell you about my fancies, but sometimes when I look at the park, as it is now, in the summer heat, I think I shall meet the midday spook. Other countries have ghosts at midnight, but I always thought there was something more sensible in our way. The strong light burning down like this – there is something terrifying about it. More uncanny than the darkness, if you ask me.'

'That is because you are a man of science, doctor, and not given to prejudice.'

'Well, perhaps. Maybe I am rational. But then, there was Voltaire and he was enlightened too, and in one of his plays he made a ghost appear at noon in full daylight and it was a washout and nobody felt creepy. He should have been completely on the side of reason and left the spooks alone. One can't have it both ways. And this goes for me, too. I kiss your hand, dear madam.'

CHAPTER 17

IT WAS three o'clock in the afternoon. Standing at one of
the French windows in the octagon room, Raoul Marek
looked at the park with the feeling of delight and distrust
which had moved him ever since his first day in Kirna.

In the far distance the massed foliage stretched a peacock
blue drapery across the azure. In the foreground the cherub
stood above the fountain like a pearl risen above its shell.
Behind him, the old lady picked out a tune by Haydn on the
piano, a mere trickle of a melody. A nervous laughter rose
in his throat. It really was too much of a good thing: in
front of him the park with no more reality than a stage prop
for a rococo scene; behind him the simpering, painted landscape on the walls and, to complete it all, this air like that
from an eighteenth-century musical box.

He lit a cigarette and felt soothed by the acrid taste. He
was not sincere enough to admit to himself that it was not
the make-believe of a past century which shattered his com-
posure, but a feeling that he did not fit in.

He had visited the kitchen garden in the morning and had
been more at his ease. He had experienced the satisfaction

which some natures derive from beholding neatness and order: the sharply defined beds, the straight rows of plants, all of equal height and width, the evenly trimmed shrubs and the espalier trees with their branches symmetrically flattened against the trelliswork. The memory of it cheered him up. He went to Bettine, who stood by the inlaid ebony table, turning the leaves of an album.

'I say,' he said, 'I had quite an adventure this morning. I met the lady in black, Aunt Louise, if I may call her so. I have heard about her since I came here, of course, and I always think of her as Aunt Louise. I can't help it.'

'I am sure we should all like to make you a present of her, if it were possible. But please go on.'

'I met her with two carrots. I mean, she was holding them in her hand. It was in the kitchen garden. She stopped me. She called me by my name. I was rather staggered. I did not think she was so well informed. I had thought she had eyes for the windfalls only.'

'Oh no,' answered Bettine. 'She takes what is called a keen interest. So long as it does not cost her anything.'

'Oh, I see. She told me that my father had been her partner at dancing classes. Although you would not think so now, she said. I did not know what to answer, so I admired her carrots.' He began to giggle. 'She told me she was going to grate them and put them in a cake mixture. It saves eggs.'

He flopped with both arms on the table and shook with laughter. Bettine smiled.

'Of course,' she said. 'Poor Aunt Louise has to save eggs, because we have only about three hundred a day. I remember, when I was a child and mama was still on speaking terms

152

with her, she would offer me chocolates and tell me at the same time that she hoped I knew that it was very impolite to accept anything, when paying a visit. And yet' – she grew serious again – 'at our birthdays she used to give us extremely expensive presents. Strange, isn't it? But when we got them she always said: This is really much too good for a child of your age. I hope your mother will lock it away and keep it for you.'

Raoul Marek lit a cigarette. 'You know, Miss Bettine, I want to tell you something. I hope you won't think it queer, but I'll explain. When I heard today that your niece – Mrs. Ritter, I mean, because you are much too young to be an aunt – that she was ill, I was glad. It's nothing serious I heard and of course I was glad. I was glad because she is ill and it's nothing serious. One cancels out the other, more or less, and yet it has happened and it makes it all right. You see, it's rather strange and I don't know how to put it, but ever since I came to Kirna I felt all wrong in my skin, if you know what I mean. Everything gave me the creeps and made me jumpy. The silliest things; you'd laugh if I told you. It's probably because everything is so old here and is full of history, or if not actual history, at least all sorts of happenings, I should imagine; so that the whole time I had this queer presentiment that something dreadful was going to happen. And now something has happened. I mean an illness out of the blue like this and so unexpected – it isn't as if she was old or ailing or anything – well, it's a tremendous relief, you know.'

'I quite understand,' replied Bettine. 'I never have any presentiments myself, but these things exist.' She idly turned a page of the album. 'It's a pity Margot has to stay in bed.

The boys will be here very soon. And she is very fond of them. You have met them, haven't you? They are not as bad as they would like to make one believe. The youngest, Lolo, has a quite scholarly brain, although he hides it very well. He used to write poems in Latin. But then, in these surroundings, it is difficult. We were always taught that it isn't clever to be clever. Clever boys are supposed to be bores and clever girls frighten the men away.'

She surveyed him with an expression which he could not make out. He had the conviction, as so often before, since he had come to the castle, that it was useless to pay her court. She was friendly, helpful and tactful in a withdrawn way, and there was always a chill and a reserve in her behaviour. There was always a hint that she had thoughts of her own and that they were not very complimentary towards her surroundings. But then, he reflected, the whole lot of them were disconcerting. His hostess came out with startling remarks between tinkling on the piano and spells of crochet-work. Mr. Birk with all his bluff and harmless talk had made him feel uncomfortable on many occasions. He felt in an obscure way that this family had grown up like the park, hiding the past beneath its silent shade.

There was a cough and a knock at the door. Emma came in with a slight rustle of starched linen; she wore her black and white like an armour.

'The young gentlemen have arrived, madam. Mr. Birk is taking them up. I have arranged for the coffee in the garden-room.'

The old lady left her piano-stool and advanced towards the middle of the room.

'Don't let Ruzena wait on us,' she said quietly. 'Send up Vlasta or Mila or whomever you like. Ruzena gets so flustered when they untie her apron the whole time. I don't have to tell you.'

'Certainly not, madam . . . I know how it is.' And Emma withdrew with an eloquent glance.

Raoul Marek had risen too.

'The boys can be very exasperating,' said the old lady. 'But I believe that there is always a way out to avoid these things. When I was young, my brother Gustav – he was killed in the war – tried to annoy me every time after the parents had left the dining-room. I knew that if I went out past him, he would tug at my hair and I would slap his face and we would have a regular dog-fight. So I went out by another door without getting near him. We cannot change human nature, Mr. Marek, but we can consider it.'

'Absolutely, Mrs. Birk-Borovec.'

The boys of Semtin burst in like an invasion of three times the number which they actually were. Mr. Birk and Alice made up the rear, together with an aged black dachshund.

As they charged towards the old lady, Bettine said in a low voice: 'I am so glad they have only brought the small dog with them. Their huge beasts frighten me, you know. They leap up and put their paws on your shoulders and you are thrown down before you know where you are. For your information, this animal is called Max. It is really Aunt Mila's dog; her husband's name is Max and one of the sons is called Max and I leave it to your imagination why she gave the dog this name. It can be interpreted in different ways.'

'Oh quite, absolutely,' answered Raoul Marek, and he watched the three young men, sleek and white clad, as they stepped up to the old lady, one behind the other and kissed her extended hand. Then they shook hands with Bettine and the young man, obviously bored already by so much polite exertion.

'Uncle Tony told us to leave Rex and Rollo at home,' said Jenda. 'For your sake, Bettine. You always were a cry-baby. But you don't know what you have missed. I taught them a new trick – a capital trick. I could show it on the stage. It's like this. I spit up right in the air – like this –' and he sent a blob of saliva towards the ceiling – 'and Rollo catches it in his mouth.'

Bettine quailed.

'Jenda,' exclaimed Alice, 'you are disgusting. You are not fit to be in a drawing-room. Look at the mess.'

'Where, Alice?' asked Jenda innocently and put his foot over the offending spittle.

'Right on the floor.'

'Where? You can't see it now, can you, Alice?'

'No,' replied Alice with a smile which she tried to suppress.

'Then what are you making the fuss about?'

She shrugged and went to another group which had assembled round the old lady.

'Everybody sends their love,' said Lolo.

'How is your father?' asked Mrs. Birk-Borovec. 'Still the blood pressure?'

'Oh, yes, but he enjoys it now. He threw out the doctor who told him to cut out drink and cigars. Now he has gone back to Doctor Torek. The old boy tells him exactly the same, but when the consultation is over they retire into father's office and drink and smoke their heads off together.'

'Any more news?'

'Max set the curtains on fire to see how they would burn. Mother is livid. Father stopped his pocket-money for a week.'

'No more throwing ducks and drakes, eh, you wasters?' guffawed Mr. Birk. His nephews had a remarkable skill in this pursuit, sometimes making the stone leap as often as fifteen times in the water. Usually, instead of throwing with a flat pebble, they practised with five-Crown pieces.

Max, who had up to then been listening to the epic of his exploits with a modest air, plucked a branch off a green trailing plant from a carved and gilded wall bracket and draped it round his head like a wreath.

'I don't give a damn about the pocket-money,' he announced. 'The old man will simmer down again. I am steeling myself against the blows of fortune, Aunt Ida. Like the Roman emperor. May they hate if only they fear, you know. And nobody's master and nobody's slave. I say, I am terribly hungry. Will there be anything decent to eat?'

'Will there be anything decent! Of course there will, you greedy rapscallion. Who d'you think we are? Archdukes or what? We are not so high up yet, my boy, as to be able to give plain bread and butter. Not by a long chalk yet.'

Mr. Birk drew up an armchair and sat down astride on it with his arms clasping the back.

'Don't you snigger at me, you abortion of a Roman emperor you, I know what I am talking about. Remove the parsley from your head and listen. When I was in England

157

the last time, in – let me see – well, anyway, yes, that's it. Before I got my groom Robinson. We were still speaking with Louise, I remember; she saw me off at the station in Prague, so it must have been in nineteen and four. I stayed with Lord Kirkwood at the time, in Cranby Hall. He was master of the otter hounds, very nice man, too, got the right ideas about everything and all that. Then he threw a big do, the hunt ball. Now wipe this grin off your face. When I say big, I mean big. There I was, plain Tony Birk from somewhere in Bohemia – that's where the gypsies come from, so they think in England, and I'm blessed if they did not think I should prance about with a fiddle and tell their fortune and give them fleas, only they were too polite to say so. So there I was, and there they were, milling round me, the best blood from the best stables in the county. Most of them had plain names and no title, but that does not mean anything over there – it's blue blood just the same. When we got down to supper, it looked all right, mind you. The usual things, cold pheasant in aspic and a saddle of venison and a ham with a frill and with it the footmen with powdered hair and silk breeches – all picked for their shapely legs; he did things well, did Lord Kirkwood. I got down a bit late, don't know why any more. The buffet looked like a battlefield. Never mind, I think, I will have a sandwich. So I take one and have a bite. And what d'you think it was? Lettuce, my boys. Good old lettuce. Not lobster, not salmon, not caviare. Lettuce my boys. I thought, well, damn it, of all the impertinence. Hunt ball and county and powdered flunkeys and lettuce. How dare they? But then I sat down and did a bit of thinking and pulled myself together. Tony, I said to myself, there is a lesson for you. Lord Kirkwood is a peer of the realm and if he likes to stuff his sandwiches with lettuce, he can do so. It's his good right and you are honoured to eat it. But if you were to give your guests lettuce at a ball, that would be an insult. So I went back to Kirna. It was not the only thing I learnt in England, let me tell you. We must know our place, boys. Then I went upstairs and played parlour games and won the white enamel clock which is in Ida's bedroom.'

There was cheering and laughter. Emma came in and said contemptuously that the coffee was served. Jenda slithered towards her across the floor and caught her round the waist. 'Emma, my lovely Emma,' he cried, 'do you still love me?' She ignored him and looked steadily above his head. 'It's in the garden-room, madam.'

'Jenda,' said Alice, 'have you no sense of decency left? What if your mother saw you now?'

'She'd say, thank heaven, for once somebody nice and steady, Alice.'

'Mama, will you please exert your influence?'

'Come here, Jenda,' said the old lady, unmoved. 'Come and carry my bag. And my shawl.'

'Very well, Aunt Ida. Only because it's you. You are still the most beautiful woman in the family. I don't care what anybody says.'

At last everybody was ready to go downstairs, hindered by Max the dachshund, who had the regrettable habit of squeezing himself through the door simultaneously with the others, and who tried to precede each member of the family at the same time.

Alice addressed herself to Emma, who was following behind: 'And see to it that the young gentlemen don't drink their coffee too black, Emma; it's poison for young people, and they are excitable enough as it is.'

In the middle of the meal Lolo got up and declared that he wanted to see his beautiful cousin.

'Which one do you mean, you low character?' shouted Mr. Birk. 'Bettine is right next to you and you have got Alice straight opposite.'

'I mean Margot, Uncle Tony. Alice and Bettine are beautiful, of course, each in her own way, but so is Margot. In her own way, too, that is.'

'You can all go up afterwards and say hallo,' said Alice. 'But only for five minutes. Doctor Torek said no excitement.'

The boys shrieked and whistled. 'The family is never exciting, Alice.'

'Anyway, I am going up now,' said Lolo and pushed his chair back. He helped himself to a canapé with Russian salad and slices of hard-boiled egg and put several cheese straws behind one ear.

'Lolo, sit down at once,' said Alice. 'It isn't proper. And besides, I don't understand this sudden eagerness. Only a few years ago you used to come along in your riding-boots and sit down on the library floor and smash all Margot's doll china.'

'It served her right. The library is not a place for knick-knacks. Decent people keep books in it, the way my old man does. He's got time-tables there going forty years back and all the classics and all his old account books. And now I'm off. Come on, Max.'

160

The dog crawled out from beneath the table and looked at him, showing the whites of his eyes.

'Mama!' exclaimed Alice. 'I appeal to you.'

'What am I to do with him, Alice? I can't tie him to the chair,' answered the old lady and dipped a sponge finger into her cup.

'You can trust the boy,' shouted Mr. Birk. 'What are you worrying about, Alice? And if he burns down the curtains, the room will be all the lighter for it, haha.'

'That was Max, Uncle Tony; please don't be unfair.' With this, Lolo walked away from the table, sauntered past the marble console and stepped out on the terrace. The dachshund kept by his side with a lopsided gallop and his ears streaming in the air.

For a short while everybody continued silent, eating and drinking with that quiet assiduity which is the sign that the food is being enjoyed.

From time to time a gust of breeze ran through the ivy leaves which fringed the arches and their shadows trembled over the painted cockatoos and the silvered dolphin.

Close to the side-table stood Emma, her figure firmly outlined against the blue summer air and framed by the pillared archway. Planted as she was, on the black and white lozenged marble floor, it seemed as though she had sprung from it, with her black and white attire and her stony attitude. Two young maids were hovering about, balancing platters and breathing heavily.

Mr. Birk helped himself to one of those twisted and hollow rolls of light yellow and porous texture, filled with strawberry cream, which are called 'corkscrew curls' in that part of Bohemia. 'Come on, everybody and say something,' he exclaimed. 'What's the matter with the whole lot of you? Struck by lightning, or what? I suppose Alice is listening for yells from Margot's room. Own up, Alice.'

'No, she does not, Uncle Tony,' replied Jenda. 'That's just the trouble. Margot is not the kind of girl who yells.'

'*Je vous en prie, pas devant les servantes,*' said Alice, who like all women of her class had acquired foreign languages for such occasions.

'These cakes and things are all very well, Ida,' remarked Mr. Birk. 'But where are the pineapples, eh? Must we all wait for them till Oscar turns up? And what if he does not come soon and they will be rotten? Have you thought of it?'

'What would you rather have, Uncle Tony, no Oscar and no pineapples or Oscar and pineapples?' asked Max. 'Or pineapples without Oscar?'

'I propose,' shouted Jenda, 'that we send a deputation upstairs to Margot. It's for her to decide. Anyone who wants to place bets can do so now with me.'

'Wait for Lolo and see what he says,' said Mr. Birk. 'He is coming back; I can hear him.'

'Let's hide the cakes first; we'll tell him they are finished and that we have left,' shrieked Jenda. 'Quick.'

He snatched two dishes from one of the maids and crawled with them under the table. His brother handed him two more and, clutching a silver basket with a criss-cross pyramid of sponge fingers, disappeared to join him. The table heaved.

'You are upsetting the coffee!' cried Alice. 'Come out at once.'

A hand pinched her leg under the tablecloth. 'Shut up, Alice,' hissed a voice. 'Don't be a spoilsport.'

Mr. Birk slapped his thigh and laughed uproariously. Alice gave a stifled moan. Raoul Marek tried to suppress his giggles and dabbed some stains of coffee spattered on his coat, while Bettine signalled beneath the table, beckoning them to come out. The old lady wiped her mouth and turned her head towards the terrace, as Oscar Ritter came in.

Breathless and walking very fast, he sank on the tattered chair next to the marble console. He threw his head back and closed his eyes for a second. Then he got up and approached the table with an offended air. He kissed the old lady's hand and glanced round. There was an eloquent silence.

'I threw myself into the car and flew to Kirna,' said Mr. Ritter with a suspicious look. The table heaved and rolled and from it issued noises like a running motor and the blowing of a horn. He jumped back and gripped the old lady's chair. The company was shaking with laughter.

'Have a cake, Oscar, stuffed with coffin nails,' said a sepulchral voice and a dish rose in the air. Then, amidst the general uproar, Max and Jenda emerged from their hiding-place.

'What a happy surprise, Oscar!' exclaimed Alice and threw furious glances on the boys. 'Come and give me a kiss. Have you had coffee yet? You must be fatigued after the journey.'

'I snatched some coffee on the way, but I could not drink it – it was horrible. And I am tired, of course. I threw myself into the car and flew here, as soon as I had the message.'

He kissed her lightly on the forehead and remained by her side with an expression of suffering and astonishment.

'I don't understand,' he remarked. 'I thought Margot was ill.'

'So she is Oscar, so she is,' roared Mr. Birk with rollicking good humour. He guffawed and slapped his thigh and a new fit of laughter shook everybody with the exception of Alice.

'We were actually just talking of you, before you came in,' said Jenda with an innocent face. 'Talk of the devil.'

'Don't take any notice of them,' said Alice. 'And please sit down and make yourself comfortable. The boys are impossible; they always are. The only thing is to ignore them. I am sure you want some coffee. Have you had coffee yet?'

'I told you a minute ago; if you had only listened.'

'I am so sorry, of course. It's the boys. They are so very trying. Emma, a chair for Mr. Ritter. And a cup. You might have thought of it yourself, Emma. Emma. . . .'

But Emma had gone.

CHAPTER 18

UPSTAIRS IN in the 'yellow room' Margot was sitting up in bed. With her abundant ash blonde hair tumbled over the pillow and the silk nightdress sprigged with tiny flowers and a black velvet ribbon threaded round the neck-line revealing her smooth and white shoulders, she had an air of make-believe innocence and child-of-nature which was as charming as it was absurd.

Lolo was sitting on the bed with one foot tucked under him and the other dangling down. They were both smoking cigarettes and inhaling in small and sharp gulps.

'You are sitting very pretty here, I must say,' remarked Lolo. 'Peace and quietness and roses all around you. What more do you want?'

'Nothing, Lolo. Although the roses get on my nerves a bit. You should see my bedroom in Prague. Venetian baroque, not too grand, but very distinguished at the same time.'

'But you rather prefer this, just the same, don't you, or you would not be here?'

'This is a leading question, Lolo.'

165

'Where have you got this expression from? From that Raoul who is a lawyer?'

She pouted. 'No. I don't know.'

He put his cigarette out. 'He looks an ass to me. And a dandy. A dandy and an ass.' He took out a fresh cigarette and lit it. 'But so am I.'

Margot touched his sleeve. 'What has come over you, Lolo?'

'Can't say. One cannot be a clown all the time. Still, there is nothing else left to me. Every day I do the rounds on the farm and I look at the cows and they look back at me. It's better to laugh about it than to cry, isn't it?'

'Don't talk like this, Lolo. In your mood you can say this about everything in life and make it depressing. But I am ill and you should cheer me up. Do you remember that lovely trick of yours, how you used to blow a whole row of smoke rings in a straight line and spit through them?'

'Yes, I remember,' he replied moodily. He bent his head and stroked her fingertips, which lay on the bed-cover.

'Well, couldn't you?'

'No, I could not. I told you before. I am not a clown and not a performing dog either. And these tricks grow stale. You are amazingly childish. Nobody would believe you were a married woman.'

'I sometimes don't believe it myself. Do you ever get that feeling when you are at a party or in a crowd in the street and you suddenly say to yourself: Why am I here? What am I doing here? That is how I feel so often nowadays.'

'Yes, I know it,' he replied. They looked at each other in silence.

166

'What are they up to downstairs?' asked Margot. 'Still drinking coffee?'

'Yes. For ever and ever. Do you wish they'd come up? Do I bore you?'

'No, not really. Everything is so quiet. Where is Max?'

Lolo got up and took a look round the room. Then he crouched down and saw the dachshund lying beneath the washstand, holding between his front paws a sponge-bag from which he tore strips with quick and silent jerks of his head.

He returned to the bed and sat down again. 'He is busy with your sponge-bag; that's what keeps him quiet. When you can't hear and see Max, it is always a bad sign. If one has a pleasure one is grateful and discreet. Don't cry, Margot. Oscar will buy you a new one.'

'You should, Lolo. It is your animal.'

'I protest, Margot. There are certain privileges which belong to the husband only. I am sure Alice has told you.'

'And she has also told me that you are a——' She drew her breath in as she heard a tap outside.

The door flew open and Emma came in on tiptoes.

'Emma, you disappoint me,' exclaimed Lolo. 'Where is your usual tact? You come up here like a whirlwind.'

'This is no time for being tactful, Mr. Lolo. Mr. Oscar has just arrived and I suppose you'd better go downstairs and stay there.'

'What a pity, Emma. And I was admiring Margot among the roses. So you think I should go down, Emma?'

'It is not for me to think thoughts of my own, Mr. Lolo; I only thought you would prefer it yourself.'

167

She stepped to the bedside table and swept a few cake crumbs into the hollow of her hand. Then she piled up the used coffee-set and plates on a small oval silver tray, lifted it up shoulder high on her fingertips and straightened with the other hand the cloth on the table.

On her way out she paused for a second. 'The new sponge-bag. Dear me. Like master like dog.'

'Do you still love me, Emma?' asked Lolo absentmindedly. She closed the door.

'She is quite right,' he added. 'Still, what will you?' He shrugged. 'Well, so long. I kiss your hand, Margot. Max! Come out from there.'

He sauntered towards the door, giving the dog a kick as he passed him.

Margot sank lower down on the pillows. She had grown pale. For a while she listened to the sound of receding foot-steps. Then she gazed in front of her for a long time.

Oscar Ritter rapped on the door, came into the room without waiting for a reply and went straight to his wife's bedside.

He was a man in his early forties, tall and well built, with quick and gauche movements. His features were drawn, the nose and cheek bones prominent, the eyes small, intelligent and deep set. Yet despite the sharpness of his face and his thinning brown hair, he would have looked younger than his age if it had not been for his habitual expression of care and anxiety. His appearance was expensive and untidy. He kept a valet, but did not look it; his hair was never sleek, his coat never spotless, his trousers never smooth.

'Ah, here you are,' he said breathlessly. 'I wanted to come

168

up immediately, of course, but I had to *faire acte de présence* downstairs and have my time wasted with those idiot boys. Margot, darling.'

He bent down and kissed her forehead, her eyes, her mouth. She turned her head away.

'Please, Oscar, close the door. You have left it open.'

'Must you say this just now?'

'I am sorry, Oscar, but there is a draught. And I am not quite well, as you know.'

'I have been looking forward to a quiet sit-down. I am dead tired. Still. There you are. I have closed it. Now say thank you, darling.' He returned to the bed and took her hand and kissed it. Then he began to kiss her arm up to the elbow.

'I am so glad to see you so well,' he said. 'I had quite a fright when they phoned me. I simply threw myself into the car and flew to Kirna.'

He paused, drew a deep breath and passed a hand over his forehead.

'Did you have a nice trip?' asked Margot. She drew her hand away and twisted a strand of hair round her finger.

'Nice? How can you ask such a thing? I am telling you I feel exhausted. There was some trouble in the refinery, nothing serious, but still. I won't tell you just now, when you are not well. And the chauffeur had his day off, so they sent me another one and he was a half-wit. First he ran over a goose, quite unnecessary, of course; he could have foreseen it happening. I did not pay for it, though. I told him to drive straight on. Then he lost his way twice. Read the map and lost his way. I always thought Tonin was not bright, but

169

this man is a moron. There are no limits to human stupidity. Naturally, if I had been in a better state myself, I would have given him more directions. But I was too exhausted. You are looking very well, though, I must say.'

'Yes, I know, Oscar. You say that in such a way as though it were a reproach. It is a local strain on the muscles or the ligaments, I am not quite sure which. If it was not for that, I would be quite fit.'

'Well, that's something. But don't you think you could have made an effort and come back to Prague? Don't you think you could have shown some consideration? I had to entertain business friends last night and there is more to come next week. And I have been sleeping very badly.'

'I am sorry, Oscar. But I could not move at all this morning. I wanted to come back, of course. It has been very tiresome.'

'I quite agree. At least you admit it. But there you are talking all the time about yourself and you still have not enquired how I am. You are really peculiar. I don't know what to think. Sometimes I think you don't care for me at all.'

He took her hand and peered at her with a vexed and tender expression.

'I am sorry, Oscar. I was just going to ask why you did not sleep well.'

'I don't really know. I had this worry on my mind with the factory. I felt more and more awake and I did not want to take a sleeping drug. In the end, at four in the morning I took one; I could stand it no longer. I would have liked some tea, but I was all alone, so I had to go without it. And then in the morning, I felt like poisoned, because I had not slept it all off, you see. I had hardly any breakfast. I felt quite faint. I don't know how I got here. I have only had five hours' sleep, you know.'

'You will make up for it tonight, Oscar. The fresh country air. Everybody sleeps here like a top.'

'Is that all you have got to say?' He rose and went to the window. He drummed on the pane. 'That is the sort of remark you might throw to anybody. To Emma – or any person who does not matter. Don't you think you could have said something nicer to me? Something which shows that you really care?'

He turned round. 'Why don't you say anything? Now you are in a bad mood again. I should like to know why. Can't you look a bit happier, just to please me? You are incredibly touchy. It is that schoolgirl silliness of yours.'

He pressed his lips together and threw his head back. His eyes returned to the window.

'Ah,' he sighed in an exalted way. 'The park. Sheer poetry. I could almost say a lyrical landscape. So opposed to what we saw in Italy, isn't it?'

'Yes,' said Margot. 'There everything was more hard and dramatic.'

'You are right. All of a sudden you understand me, completely. A minute ago you were so cold. You are a strange creature. I never know what to think of you. It's funny that you should have so much appreciation of beauty. I mean the right appreciation. Because your family certainly have not got it. When I look at this fountain, for instance – the wide dignified basin and the playfulness of the cherub – such a piquant contrast, don't you think? But if I took it away over-night and put up a garden dwarf in its place, your people would not think twice about it.'

He began to pace up and down, casting disapproving and suspicious glances at the walls, the washstand, the wardrobe.

'When I look at this room, this rose-littered horror,' he continued, 'and then at this dream of a park, I can't under-stand how people can live like this. Such beauty and such ugliness. As I said, I often wonder where you get it from.'

Margot looked at him from beneath lowered eyelids. 'My grandfather was good at drawing, Oscar. He used to tell me fairy tales and illustrate them at the same time. And he collected Chinese prints and the miniatures which are in the dining-room.'

'Ah, bah. Don't mention the miniatures. I would not give you a hundred crowns for them.'

Oscar Ritter was a man of taste and proud of it, as he was proud of all his possessions and assets. His was an academic good taste, acquired laboriously during many years; like many businessmen, he felt a respect for art, for the great and recognized works of art, and for the prices they command at auctions and sales. It was difficult to say at what point this esteem had changed into pleasure and admiration, or, to be more exact, to what degree it still existed. There was nothing spontaneous in his predilection, and like any good man of affairs, who avoids taking unnecessary risks, he only appreci-ated where well-known connoisseurs and critics before him had prepared the ground. Thus in Italy, as Margot remem-bered now, every new scenery which opened before his eyes had evoked his exalted sighs, every group of trees, hills, farmyards. Whereas driving through the neighbourhood of Kirna he never paid attention, as it was well known that this part of the country was not interesting. She watched him moving to and fro with that feeling of guilt and exasperation which she nearly always experienced in his presence.

He suddenly came to a standstill. 'What's that – mess?' he demanded and pointed with his chin to the floor by the washstand. 'Your grandmother's maids are an abomination. The real country servants. Superstitious and filthy and when they see a cockroach they cross themselves and do nothing about it. And all this idiotic devotion to their masters – this eternal curtseying and hand kissing, it always gets on my nerves when I come here. They even do it when they don't get a tip. But cleaning up? Heaven forbid. Really, your family!'

Margot sat up in bed. 'Please, Oscar. You are going too far.'

'Why shouldn't I say it? It is true, isn't it?'

'It is not true. And even if it was, you have no right to say so. This on the floor has nothing to do with anybody. I had the dog up for a while, the old dachshund. The boys brought him from Semtin. And he must have torn my sponge-bag from the hook while I did not look, and demolished it.'

Mr. Ritter remained in front of the washstand and shook his head. 'I don't know,' he said. 'They'll come to a bad end yet. Every time they come they descend upon the place like a plague of locusts. I cannot understand the old lady. If I was in her place I would forbid them the house.'

'We are all fond of them, Oscar.'

'Yes. Of course you are. Because their destructive spirit pleases you. Let it slide. Let it slide and *à la bonne heure*. You all think it smart not to care about one's possessions. How many hours do you think one of my workmen has to work before he could pay the price of such a bag?'

'Oh, Oscar, don't make such a to-do about it. They are young and full of fun and they don't mean any harm.'

He went to her bed and sat down. 'You don't deceive me, Margot; I can read you like a book. You are pleading for them because you are really defending yourself. You have got that streak as well. Do you ever care when a glass is broken or a towel gets lost?'

'I don't want to hear any more about it. I can go without a sponge-bag. Or mother will buy me one.'

'And if she does, it will come out of my money, just the same. Now, don't make such a face. It's true, isn't it?' He paused. 'You are such a moody creature, Margot. Look at me.'

She glanced up with tears in her eyes.

'You look so sweet in this nightdress. I chose it for you in Milan, do you remember? I knew it would be your style. I always think how to consider you and what would give you pleasure. And you have not told me yet that you are glad to see me.'

Without knowing it she drew the top sheet up to her chin, to cover her bare throat and shoulders.

'Of course I am, Oscar. You are very kind, I know you are. And I know I have lots of faults. But I can't help it and when you talk like this I get so depressed.'

'We won't speak about it any more. You must get a better

grip on yourself, darling. You know how much I love you, but you cannot expect me to keep my mouth shut the whole time. Look at me. I never let myself go and I have much more worries. Now give me a kiss. I have brought you a present, something very nice. It is in my small bag. Why haven't they brought up my luggage yet? Do they think I am going to sleep in the coach-house? I do not expect much from them, but Emma might have more *savoir faire*; she is the perfect servant. Never about when she is wanted. I am going out to catch her. And no more tears, darling. I don't want anybody to think that I upset you, because I am really very nice to you and you are happy, aren't you?'

He embraced her tenderly and left the room and returned a few minutes later with Emma, who, stern and blue-eyed, swam ahead of two young maids like a galleon figure on a ship's prow. He rubbed his hands and looked pleased at the sight of two suitcases and an attaché-case which reflected in their gleaming nickel locks and brown crocodile hide the rose buds on the wall paper.

'This is the first step. Now, which room am I to sleep in, Emma? Last time we were in a different wing. I feel a bit lost. The Birks shake rooms out of their sleeve like a conjurer the rabbits.'

'We changed you this time, sir, because you did not sleep well last time. On this side you only get the park and that is quiet enough. We thought you might like the room next to this one and use the adjoining chamber as a dressing-room.' Her glance swept over him contemptuously and then settled on one of the maids, who immediately straightened her bonnet.

'This thoughtfulness is amazing,' answered Oscar Ritter with an offended air. His attempt at humour had, as usual, fallen flat and, as usual, he felt annoyed about it.

'Amazing, I say,' he continued. 'When I think how in the past I was never considered at all. The way I used to be called for breakfast when you must have known that I had spent a bad night. I won't say any more about it. Show me my room.'

'Yes, sir.' Emma held a door open for him. The two young maids followed with the luggage.

'Put it down,' said Oscar Ritter. 'Leave those suitcases where they are. I said I wanted to see my room and not a word about my luggage. It is always the same. What one wants to have done is never attended to and what one never asked for is rammed down one's throat.'

'Oscar,' said Margot, 'they meant well.'

'I suppose so. I always get this excuse. I should pretty well hope they did not do it on purpose; it is the least one might expect. And then you are amazed that I am worn out. This is the sort of thing I come up against all day long, even before I can settle down to real work.' He closed his eyes and passed a hand over his brow.

He stepped into the room.

It was washed in lavender blue and had thick and heavy curtains of an imitation *verdure* tapestry. From the faded streaks in the material and the frequent breaks in the pattern it was evident that they had been made up and patched. The scanty furniture was of light pine and pear wood and covered with numerous white lace mats. The worn linoleum was partly concealed by two Persian rugs from which nearly all the colour and pile had been rubbed off by the footsteps of generations. An armchair of dark blue velvet, a twin to the ones in the octagon room, stood near the window. He covered his face with his hands. 'This is too much,' he murmured.

'I hope you will find it comfortable, sir,' said Emma. 'The wardrobe is a real fitted gentleman's wardrobe and the bed has a new mattress.'

He turned and faced her. 'So this is the room I get out of all the rooms in the castle. The blue walls are bad enough and worse with the blue-green curtains. But only an imbecile could have put the armchair in. Three blues in one room. Can't you feel how they scream at you? Who do you think I am? I suppose the coachman would not mind. But I do. How can I find any rest with these colours shrieking at me?'

'We put the easy chair in for you specially, sir, because there never are any soft chairs in the bedrooms. But I shall have it taken out. If I may say so, sir, I know what is good taste and fitting, but we are in the country, sir, and not so well set up as we should like to be.'

'Quite. I won't talk about it any more. Take the atrocity away.'

After the maids had gone, Oscar Ritter sat down on his wife's bed and produced a small jeweller's case. In it, embedded on yellow satin, were two earrings made of drop-shaded opals, framed in diamonds and mounted in platinum.

'You must wear these when you first get up again.' He kissed her. 'If I had known, I should have really brought you a sponge-bag.'

She coloured. She thanked him and tried them on.

'But you know, Oscar,' she said, turning her head this way and that in front of the hand mirror which she was holding. 'I thought you were a bit unkind, about that fauteuil, I mean. It was touching, I think, the way they had tried to please you.'

'Oh, nonsense, Margot. Whenever fools make a blunder, they always tell you how well they meant. It is the typical servant's answer. They never break anything on purpose and so on. And am I to make myself sick by looking at that chair, out of sheer consideration? Whoever considers me?'

CHAPTER 19

IT WAS in the late afternoon. The boys had made their good-byes with a great deal of hand kissing and bowing and departed in their gig to Semtin.

A mass of white and curly clouds stood in the sky like a flock of lambs. The birds were silent and the swallows flew low. The old lime tree on the gravel space in front of the castle filled the air with the rustling of leaves and the murmur of drowsy insects. It sounded like a faint breathing, the breathing of dying summer.

Oscar Ritter stood in the octagon room and with an india rubber erased a few pencilled moustaches with which the visitors from Semtin had seen fit to adorn shepherdesses and sheep alike on the landscape wallpaper. He felt pleased with himself. He had met the agent, who had offered to go with him through the accounts, but he had declined because it was Sunday. The agent had been grateful and impressed by this show of delicacy on Mr. Ritter's part. Oscar Ritter always made a point of scrupulously observing the leisure hours of his employees, although he did not apply this rule to himself. He owned and controlled a chain of raw-sugar factories and several sugar refineries, the second largest concern of its kind in Central Europe. The most strenuous part of his business career was over, yet he did not spare himself, as he belonged to those who believe that others cannot do a job as well as they can themselves. So he continued working, often fourteen hours a day, and only a few of his directors were expected to do the same. This, in his opinion, was a privilege, because it meant that he did not consider them to belong to the tribe of incompetent fools, like the majority of his fellow creatures.

The sherry was brought in and soon afterwards Raoul Marek entered the room. Alice came in for a moment with a harassed air, begged them not to disturb themselves, although they did not make the slightest move, and went away again.

Oscar Ritter pocketed his india rubber and made to pour out the drink.

'This is your first visit here, Mr. Marek? Light or dark? Not that it makes much difference, I am sorry to say. Still, one has to keep up pretences.'

'Light, please.'

'Here you are. And you like it, do you? It is nice and quiet, especially now that the locusts have gone. I don't know how any father can bring up his children like this. I have never come across such a case of vandalism before, that is, in peacetime. Have you?'

'Quite so. Absolutely.'

'How is business doing? I mean your business? You are taking your summer vacation now, I dare say. Have you shut up shop, so to speak, or do you take it in turns? Because you have a partner, haven't you, or am I wrong?'

'No. I mean yes. I have a partner, a senior partner. I should really say he has got me, not the other way round. We are both away, though. It is not worth staying in town at this time of the year. Everybody has gone away or pretends to.'

'Just as I thought. And your partner – what is his name now – where has he gone to?'

'To Italy, Mr. Ritter. Dr. Kramar, Robert Kramar is his name. I had a letter from him the other day. He is staying near Florence just now.'

'Ah, yes. I seem to remember. I have heard of him before. I may know him even, if I am not mistaken. You know how it is. One meets people and quickly looks away. And I have to meet so many people the whole time. Not that it leads to anything. But as I said, one has to keep up pretences.' He made a deprecatory movement with his shoulders and a modest face, a show of polite make-believe which takes no one in.

Alice came in with Bettine. They were both dressed in flowered stuffs, Bettine's patterned with vine leaves on a white ground, while Alice wore black chiffon with a discreet design of grey poppies and a string of pearls framing her severe neckline. Raoul Marek noticed with amusement that her whole appearance was imbued with an elderly elegance. She was, he thought, of about the same age as her daughter's husband. No doubt she was trying to look like a mother-in-law.

'I have just been upstairs to see Margot,' she exclaimed. 'Really, Oscar, you are much too generous. Those gorgeous earrings. Yes, gorgeous is the right word for them. You are spoiling the child. I have not seen such beautiful opals for ages. Although, I must say, they are perhaps a trifle too sedate for her.'

'I take the hint, Alice,' replied Mr. Ritter and kissed her hand with a show of gallantry. 'But you will have to wait till Christmas. Unless, of course, you fall ill in the meantime. . . . Now what can I do for you at present? Some sherry? Light or dark?'

'Dark, please, Oscar. And dark for Bettine, too. And your room is comfortable, you think?'

'It should be, Alice. Because it has not got good looks, so it should make up for it with comfort, if I may say so. But don't let us talk about it. Emma tells me that there is a new mattress on the bed. That does not mean, of course, that it is a good one.'

'I do hope you will sleep well,' replied Alice and took a sip with an anxious face.

'I think I will. I am sure I will. I can feel it. It is queer you know. There are times when I am completely certain that I shall have a good night's rest and it always comes true. There are other times when I cannot tell – could be and could not be, you know, and then it varies. And on other occasions again, when I had a great upset, for instance, I feel quite sure that I shall never close an eye and I am always right in these cases again.'

Raoul Marek brought a dish with salted almonds to the ebony table at which Bettine had seated herself, and decided to stay with her till dinner. He could hear snatches of Mr. Ritter's talk; he was discussing his physician in Prague and another doctor whom he had consulted. 'I think he is good.

182

He makes mistakes sometimes, but that is only to be expected. And he is intelligent enough to admit it, not like the other fools who make silly excuses and blame my disposition and temperament and heaven knows what besides.'

Bettine asked the young man if he would like to see the fair in the village.

'We are all going this evening,' she said. 'My sister and Uncle Tony. And some of the maids are coming as well. What a pity Margot is laid up; she loves that sort of thing. I am not very good at it. The roundabout makes me seasick, but I like to look on. Those vehicles done up like swans and lions and chariots are splendid, aren't they?'

'I have not been to a fair for years,' replied the young man. 'Is Emma going as well?'

'Oh no. Not she. That sort of thing is beneath her, as you can imagine. She thinks it is a lovable whim on our part to go and to pretend that we enjoy it. A reversed snobbery, so to speak.'

'Will there be any gingerbread hearts?'

'Of course, Mr. Marek. We always buy them, and then cook is offended, because she says she can make much better gingerbread, and so we daren't eat them.'

They talked about gypsies and fortune-telling and related experiences which had happened to people they knew and devised possible and plausible explanations as one usually does and which is the price paid by educated people when they divert themselves with the supernatural.

It did not seem long before they went in to dinner. The dining-room looked more festive than usual. The big oil lamp hanging from a brass chain had been pulled up higher towards the ceiling; at the head and foot of the table white wax candles burnt in old-fashioned silver candelabra. Their flames were mirrored on the frost-white damask and reflected in the tumblers, which had stripes of milky and clear glass and bore large engraved initials. The table was more richly laid than was customary, with red and white wine glasses and chalices for dessert wine, and in front of each cover stood a silver salt cellar and a cut-glass dish with butter curls.

Raoul Marek saw it with amusement, and remembering the incident of the coat-hangers, was in no doubt as to the reason for this opulence.

Oscar Ritter sat on the right-hand side of the old lady, Mr. Birk on her left. The cold soup was served in cups of Dresden china, which with their naïvely painted flowers brought a breath of summer into the cold and snowy sparkle of silver, glass and damask linen.

'It is a pity you were not here yesterday, Oscar,' said Mr. Birk as he unfolded his napkin. 'We were very enterprising. Went to Boleslav and saw the sights there, new relic and all. Good success, wasn't it, Ida?'

'Oscar is not interested, Tony,' replied the old lady.

'That is not the right word for it,' said Mr. Ritter. 'Interested – everything can be interesting. But when it comes to religion, I am disgusted. Not with religion itself, of course, but with the claptrap which has accumulated around it. This emphasis on Christ's wounds, for instance. And his blood which saved us. I find it revolting. It turns my stomach. The same with the martyrs, the way they

184

kissed leprous sores and gloried in it. I cannot bear the thought of it. It encourages people to be unhygienic. Why don't they invent a saint who washed his hands before every meal and gargled before going to bed?'

The next course was hot lobster in a white sauce.

'I love lobster,' said Mr. Ritter after the first few mouthfuls. 'But it is all spoilt for me. I like it in the shell. Why did they have to take it out and mess it up? Half of the pleasure is gone.'

'Would you rather I took it away, sir?' enquired Emma, who stood behind his chair.

'That will do. Will you please attend to the wine, Emma,' exclaimed Alice, who sat next to him. 'If Mr. Ritter wants to have it taken away he will say so.'

'It does not really matter,' remarked Oscar Ritter, with a face which expressed that it mattered very much. 'Thank you, Emma. Leave it. I will eat it now I have started. I don't like waste. Besides, it is not bad, of course; it is only not as good as it might have been.'

'I am very sorry, Oscar,' said Alice and played nervously with her string of pearls. She cast a furious look at Emma. 'I will remember it, though. It will not happen again, I promise you that. I can assure you——'

'Don't make such a to-do, Alice,' shouted Mr. Birk. 'If you go on like this, Oscar will think it is a tragedy and we will have to be the chorus and weep into our napkins, haha.'

'Don't be absurd, Uncle Tony. You believe in being hospitable as much as anybody else does.'

'Of course I do, hang it all; I like to see our guests being comfortable. But Oscar is; you only don't understand it. He does not like to suffer in silence, do you, Oscar my boy? But when he can talk about it he works it off and all is forgiven and forgotten. And that's as it should be. A good horse never sulks long either. Now, what I want to know, Ida, when are we going to get anything to eat? I am starving. What is this I see? An ox in his dressing-gown? Hahaha. Eh?'

It was a dish of roast beef á la Wellington, one of the culinary prides of Castle Kirna, a long and lean cut off the loin, baked in a wrapping of puff pastry and accompanied by a sauce Remoulade. The red wine was poured out, and after Mr. Ritter had tasted it, his eyes sought Emma, who at once came to his side.

'Take the glass, Emma,' he said, 'and just feel it. Do you consider this is *chambré* enough? I don't. The Moselle was not sufficiently iced either, but I thought I'd let it go. But this is – undrinkable. Can you take it away and do something about it?'

'Certainly, sir. I can have it warmed up in a minute.'

'Bravo, my boy,' applauded Mr. Birk. 'Speak your mind. You have more guts than I have. I am henpecked, my boy, from all sides. But you will go down in history as having braved the house-dragon.'

Mr. Ritter inclined his head with a tired smile and brushed away a few dead moths which lay on the cloth surrounding the burning candles. The old lady began to question him about his impressions in Italy.

'Of course, Italy,' he said, leant back in his chair and laid down his knife and fork.

'Gee up, we are going,' muttered Mr. Birk into Bettine's ear. Alice gave them an angry look.

'There are so many Italys,' said Oscar Ritter. 'The trouble is that they are so un-Italian – except that stretch with the renaissance, Florence to Rome, roughly speaking, of course. There is Sicily with its baroque, which is a sort of Spanish colonial style, rather like in South America. And then a strong African influence with it. On the other hand, in Apulia you get those Romanesque fortresses nobody knows. They were built by the German emperor Frederick in the twelfth century and have nothing to do with Italy. Then there is Venice, a thing by itself, mostly coloured by the Islamitic tradition and the only town in Italy which still had a living culture in the eighteenth century. But most people don't realize that, of course, they are fools. So the Germans go to Venice because they think that's Italy, and the English make their pilgrimage to Florence, which is naturally what they would do, what do you expect?'

Emma approached the table with the red wine.

'Why is this?' asked the old lady and glanced at him sideways.

'Florence is the beginning of the renaissance,' said Oscar Ritter. 'Very pure and clear and rather touching, by its immaturity, like all beginnings. That is why' – he took up his glass. which had been filled – 'they like it so much. They prefer things in the bud, because they are restrained and immature themselves.' He closed his eyes and took a gulp of red wine. 'It is much better,' he said to Emma, 'but not quite perfect unfortunately. It is now a fraction too warm.'

He shook his head and with a sigh arranged on his fork a morsel of meat, pastry and browned potato.

The old lady broke a bread roll and mopped up the yellow

sauce on her plate, heedless of Alice's reproachful glance.

'This is worth hearing,' she remarked. 'I have never been to England myself, but my husband had many connections in the City, as you know. And Tony – you can imagine that to him England is paradise. I always thought there must be something wrong with a people who have not had a revolution for several hundred years. It is not healthy.'

'Fiddlesticks, Ida!' exclaimed Mr. Birk. 'There is nothing wrong with people who hunt the fox as the English do. No other country in the world has anything like it.'

'True, Tony,' replied the old lady. 'But other countries have other things again.'

'Of course they have, Ida. I know that as well as you do. Do you think I am a fool or what?'

'Mind you,' said Oscar Ritter, addressing himself exclusively to the old lady, 'I like to be fair. This quality of the English, this restraint, this fear of letting themselves go, explains why they paint so badly and make such fine furniture. They have not got the passion and sensuality of the French or Italians. But when they make a chair, they know that it must be strong and light and comfortable. They have balance and a feeling for line and quality and they don't smother it with ornamentation. And they never make anything top-heavy.'

'That is quite true, Oscar my boy. It's all goodness with them and no flash. In other words, they are jolly good people. I have always said it all along, haven't I, Ida? And what Oscar just said about painting reminds me of Lord Kirkwood and the lettuce. What d'you say, Ida?'

'I see what you mean,' replied the old lady.

'I say,' said Raoul Marek to Bettine in a low voice, 'Mr. Ritter is fascinating to listen to. I had no idea he knew so much. Although, of course, it is not just his knowledge. It is the way he puts different things together and shows unexpected relationships. And he analyses everything with such a virtuosity.'

'Oh, quite,' she replied. 'As you say, he is very clever at pulling things to pieces. Personally, I find it entertaining when he blames Italy for being un-Italian; Italy is far away. If only he would stick to that sort of subject.'

The second meat course was a mould of iced veal paprica, chopped and blended with whipped cream, whose pink and grey marbled surface shimmered under a layer of meat-jelly. It was bordered by lemon slices cut like stars and heaped with caviare, alternating with handfuls of pickled button mushrooms tumbled into nests of curling parsley.

Mr. Ritter surveyed it with suspicion. 'I don't know if I should eat all this,' he remarked. 'It is rather late. It might interfere with my night's rest.' He helped himself sparingly.

'But you won't go to bed yet, Oscar,' said Alice. 'You have got hours in front of you. We shall not stay long at the fair and when we return we will expect to find you still up. We see you so rarely and you have not even started telling us about your trip and everything.'

'So you are going to the fair?' he asked. 'You might have at least asked me if I did not want to come along with you.'

'The children took it for granted that you would not care for it,' replied the old lady. 'We know that this sort of thing does not interest you.'

'Besides, I knew you would be too tired,' added Alice

with an expression of anxiety and solicitude.

'I don't want to go; you are quite right,' replied Oscar Ritter. 'But you might have at least made the gesture to ask me. It is not very nice to be disposed of like – a parcel. And also, if you knew that I was tired, you could have stayed at home and kept me company and I could have gone to bed early. Don't you think you might have given me a bit more thought?'

'We shall not go if you feel that way,' exclaimed Alice. 'Though we are not going for the pleasure of it; I need hardly tell you that. We must show ourselves; it is expected of us, that's all.'

'That's right, Oscar,' guffawed Mr. Birk. 'They'll all break down and sob if they don't see us there.'

'It's quite all right,' said Oscar Ritter. He closed his eyes for a second and passed a hand over his forehead. 'You must go, of course. I will keep Margot company for a while – not too long, though, because she should rest – and afterwards I shall read or something. It is of no consequence.'

The sweet was brought in, a pineapple cream lavishly decorated with crystallized fruit and shrouded in a veil of spun sugar.

'Aha, at last!' shouted Mr. Birk and slapped his thigh. 'That's thanks to you, Oscar my boy; you have brought splendour to our lowly cottage, hasn't he, Ida?'

'Really, Uncle Tony, you sometimes amaze me the way you talk,' exclaimed Alice. 'I don't know what Oscar will think.'

'Never mind what he thinks. We've got our pineapples.' He seized his glass and raised it. 'This is to you, Oscar, and many more pineapples.'

Alice continued to look disapproving, but in the end she decided to smile.

A few minutes later the old lady rose from the table.

'I think you had better be on your way,' she said. 'While there is still a gleam of daylight. And, Oscar, if you would like to go upstairs and look in at Margot, do so. I shall be in the drawing-room.'

She held out her hand to him, which he kissed, while her glance travelled above his bent head.

CHAPTER 20

THE CURTAINS were not yet drawn. The sun had gone down and the day was dying. A light still lingered outside, pale and ethereal as though drained of its life-blood.

The drawing-room lay in semi-darkness. The oil lamp burning on the satinwood table in front of the settee cast a narrow circle of brightness over the lap of the old lady, her white hands holding an open book and one of the carved sphinxes at her back.

Oscar Ritter opened the door cautiously and halted for a while.

'It's getting very dark,' he said.

'Would you like to light another lamp?'

'No, thank you.' He advanced a few steps and stopped in front of a three-winged screen which he lifted up and turned about, so that the light fell on to it. It was a fairly low screen, covered entirely with tapestry, so that no frame was showing. It had a pattern of blue and green grapes hanging over trellis-work, intermingled with brown vine leaves and tendrils.

'This is nice,' he said. 'Quite nice.'

'Emma found it in the attic the other day,' said Mrs.

Birk-Borovec. 'I liked it, so I kept it here. Would you like to sit down?'

'Thank you.' He put the screen back in its place and drew up a chair. 'I have got something very similar at home; with grapes and vines, too. Mine, of course, is antique.'

She glanced at him sideways. 'Oscar,' she said, 'will you please bring me my writing folder. Over there, on the desk.'

He got up and gave it to her.

'Thank you, Oscar.' The old lady opened it and from one of the inside flaps she drew a letter. It had a foreign stamp on it. 'This is for you,' she said. 'It came yesterday. I put it away and kept it for you. I did not want Margot to see it.'

He looked at it briefly. For a while he held it in his hand. 'Will you excuse me if I read it now?'

She nodded.

He broke the envelope and with an irritable movement brought his chair nearer to the lamp. He read and coloured for a second. Then he laid it on the table.

'This is – this is not very pleasant,' he said. 'Sheer and downright——' He rose and began to pace up and down.

'Please read it,' he said and stopped for a second in front of the old lady. Then he resumed his movement.

'I wonder,' he said, 'how much this young Marek, this lawyer, knows. At first I did not quite connect him. I drew him out a bit, and sure enough, it is his partner. But he did not let on.'

Mrs. Birk-Borovec meanwhile unfolded her lorgnon and, without paying attention to him, perused the letter with an unmoved face. Then she placed it again on the table and dropped the lorgnon into her bag. She looked up.

'I don't quite understand, Oscar. It is very good news, as far as I can see. Surely you are pleased. You should be very glad that the person got married. You always hoped she would, but did not think it could happen under the circumstances.'

'Of course I am very pleased. Exceedingly so. As you say, it surpasses my greatest hopes. But the man – he of all people. After his behaviour.'

He sank down on a chair and stroked his hair. His face dipped in shadows looked more sunken in and the bones stood out with painful sharpness. He lit a cigarette.

'I am not quite *au courant*, Oscar. If you could please explain. Of course, only if you want to. This Robert in the letter, this friend of yours——'

'He is Robert Kramar, the senior partner of that young Marek. I have known him all my life. We went to school together. He has stabbed me in the back. And to think that we went to school together.'

He continued to stroke his hair and his eyes wandered slowly round the room with a harrowed expression.

The old lady looked into the distance with unseeing eyes. 'I went to school with him. He sat at my table.' How often had she heard those protests, childish and desperate, which people utter when they have been betrayed; as though the blow could have come from anybody else except from their friends.

'I want to be quite fair, of course,' continued Oscar Ritter. 'I cannot blame Carlotta; she is ill, as you know, and her brain has been a bit affected by the disease. Not seriously, mind you, but it is dulled and blunted somehow. I noticed

194

it when I saw her just recently. Besides, it was what she wanted all along. Only to get married, at all costs. No, I cannot reproach her. Then there is her mother, old Marina, a real Italian peasant. She cannot write, she reads with difficulty, she is a primitive, strong person. Very straightforward and impulsive. She is very fond of me. There were times when she picked up a rake or a kitchen knife and went for me because she was annoyed that I would not marry Carlotta. A minute later it was all over and she would hug and kiss me and rush into her kitchen and cook my favourite dishes. That is the sort of woman she is, to give you an idea. Nothing underhand there, nothing calculating. But what am I to think? She may have acted in perfectly good faith. As a matter of fact, I am sure she did.

'Just imagine it – that will convince you. When I went down to see them a few weeks ago, I left Margot in Florence for two days and went out there to the village. Marina received me alone; Carlotta was resting, I believe. We walked up to the house through the garden. Look at this fig tree, she said to me. Do you remember fifteen years ago, when you bought the house and I moved in? I planted it myself. Look how tall it is now, and in a few years' time it will be still taller. I must say, it gripped my heart. I had planned differently when I came out there; I will tell you about it later. But when I heard this I knew that I could never ask this old woman to leave that house and that garden. I just could not. And when I left, she fell round my neck and kissed me. And she wept because I was going. Now, do you think such a person could be capable of double-crossing? She threw her arms round my neck and kissed me and she wept. She is very attached to me.'

'Forgive me, Oscar. This double-crossing you mentioned. Surely you don't blame her for having encouraged her daughter to marry your friend. You are not jealous. And you are very generous.'

He rose. 'Of course not. It's my mistake. I will explain. Perhaps you can see an angle which has escaped me. I want to be just.'

He moved his chair away from the lamp and lit a cigarette. 'As you know, I lived with Carlotta for ten years. I met her fifteen years ago. She was very young then, a beautiful child. Not very clever, not very educated; she had never had any proper schooling, poor girl; it was not her fault. She was very devoted to me. I could not marry her, of course, but I always made up for it. I looked after her and I looked after her mother. I settled Marina in the house near Florence and I don't think she could complain. Then – well, ten years is a long time – her fits got worse. She had always had them, but very few and far between. It became too much for me. She never said anything, but that look in her eyes when she regained consciousness. If only you could have seen it. It was horrible. I cannot bear the strain of having to look after a sick person. I want to be looked after myself; my state of health is not so good, as you realize. So I sent Carlotta back to Italy; it was the best thing to do. Her mother adores her and spoils her and waits on her hand and foot. I made her an allowance, of course, and there it was.'

'You behaved extremely well,' said the old lady. 'It seems the obvious thing to do and yet few men would have done it.'

'Oh, I don't know about that. And she is a sick person, unable to work for any length of time. She was very brave; she never complained about her ailment. But when I went down, once a year or so, Marina would say, the poor child, what is to become of her when I die – it moved me deeply. It was a sad business. And all the time I felt it was a bit hard on me. Other men have affairs and finish them without any trouble, and there I was with this thing on my mind, as though I had not enough worries as it is. I got married and I wanted to see the end of it. Make a clean break with Carlotta once and for all, settle a lump sum on her and wash my hands of it. Because during those last years while she was in Italy she still hoped I would take her back one day. She was so fond of me, you see. And I wanted to put a stop to it. I shirked it for quite a while; it is difficult to discuss anything serious with her. There are days when she walks about in a daze and does not understand what one says to her, and if she gets upset, she has a fit. Not very pleasant, as you see.'

'I did not know she was as ill as that,' said the old lady. 'I knew about your liaison – everybody did who knew you or knew about you; it was not a secret. But I only heard vaguely that she was delicate – no more than that.'

'Well, she does not look ill; there are no signs at all. One does not notice anything.' He got up and went to the window. 'My God, the moon,' he said in a resentful voice.

There are people who are comforted by the thought that the planets move along their course, heedless of the human fate. There are others, and Oscar Ritter was one of them,

197

who are hurt by the divine indifference and speak of the cruelty of nature.

Above the horizon the night sky was streaked with small clouds. There were no stars. The moon, almost full, stood above the fountain and in its ethereal and chilling light the park was transformed into a land of frost and glass, of snow and pearls.

Oscar Ritter beat his hand on the window-sill.

'If only I understood,' he murmured. 'I wonder what you will make of it.'

He resumed his seat. 'At last I made up my mind to take the final steps. I wrote and asked her to think it over, that perhaps she wanted to buy a shop – an antique shop or something like this, where she could potter about and earn a bit of money. Her doctor wrote, and he, too, thought it would be better for her to leave the village and live in a town, have a light occupation and see more people. I mentioned something about it in one of my letters to Carlotta and that I intended to sell the house. Because I cannot keep two separate establishments, one for Marina and one for her. Then we agreed on the date when I would come down and discuss figures and so on, and I made it quite clear that this was final and she took it very well, I thought. It worked out all right; we stopped in Florence, as I told you, and I went down there. It was quite a surprise to me to meet Robert in the house. He had known Carlotta for years, through being friendly with me, of course, but I did not know that he kept up a correspondence with her. He was taking his summer holiday, he said, and as Carlotta had written him about my decision to make a settlement on her, he had come in order to be of assistance to her in his capacity as a lawyer. I was shocked at first. It seemed queer to me. After all, it was a matter between Carlotta and me entirely, and it was nobody's business to be present. Besides, I had been supporting her for all these years out of a sense of duty, but there was no obligation to do so on my part. I was staggered. I did not like it.

'Then I thought it over and said to myself that I must be fair. Carlotta does not understand money matters and the old woman is very thrifty of course, like all peasants, but she could not grasp financial transactions either, needless to say. Perhaps it was she who wanted an adviser. You know how suspicious country people are. I bore all this in mind and unpacked; that is to say, Carlotta unpacked for me. She was as nice as ever, no bitterness at all and there were plenty of flowers in my room. I was touched to see it. It shows you how fond she is of me. Dinner was quite pleasant; I could not eat much, though. If only all goes well, I kept thinking, and she does not throw a fit.

'I slept hardly at all that night and I wished I had taken Margot with me to cheer me up a bit; but naturally that was out of the question. Then, the next day in the early afternoon we got down to it; sat down and thrashed it out. I had a great shock again. A painful surprise. I had decided, as I told you, to be more openhanded than I had intended at first and to leave the house to Marina. I made this clear to her and then I mentioned the sum which I proposed to settle on Carlotta. A very considerable amount. She can live comfortably on the interest of it without ever touching the capital. And at this point – Robert speaks up and objects.

The amount is too small in his opinion. I was thunder-struck. I stood up and said so far and no further. I was determined not to give way. You can imagine how I felt. I knew I would not have a night's rest for weeks, the way it upset me. But there was still worse to come. The old woman brought out some old letters of mine which I had written many years ago, while still living with Carlotta. Some were addressed to my bankers abroad – heaven knows how she had got hold of them. Others to some authorities. I will not tell you the details; it leads too far. Anyway, it was all in connection with travel, with foreign currency and other arrangements, and to simplify matters, I had alluded to Carlotta as my fiancée. In one letter even I had called her my wife. I don't know if you know this, but Carlotta is Italian, and in Italy the State recognizes a marriage even when it has not been legalized. They consider it as valid in cases of claims and so on, and Robert pointed out to me that on the strength of these letters Carlotta could sue me for an allow-ance due to her as my wife. Which would be an enormous amount, as you can imagine. I was forced to give in. I raised the settlement and the papers were duly signed and sealed in front of a notary. Carlotta was very nice though, all through. Afterwards we sorted out some linen and stuffs which belonged to me and which I wanted to have and she did it all for me without a murmur. She adores fine linen – I always tell Margot I wish she would look after the house-hold as well as Carlotta did. She had tears in her eyes as she folded it up for me. She had embroidered on every cloth and sheet O and C, Oscar and Carlotta, you know. And she gave it all to me. It was pathetic, really. Surely a woman who has such delicate feelings cannot do anything nasty. And the old mother. As I told you, as soon as the documents were signed she fell round my neck and kissed me. Now you know it all.'

He drew a deep breath. He lit a cigarette. His hand was shaking.

The old lady gave a sigh. 'Now I understand,' she said. 'Robert squeezed out of you as much money as he could and married it. No wonder he was so eager to protect that girl's claims. It is not a pretty story. No wonder you are upset.'

'Upset is not the word for it. Even when I think of it now, I turn pale with rage. Robert – after all, what is he? A petti-fogging lawyer – and I, one of the richest men in this country. Why should I not say it? And he did me, as though I had been a greenhorn and wet behind my ears. When I think what I did for the man. I will not count up the times I entertained him and wined him and dined him and spent pleasant hours with him; that's enough, of course, but it is not all. But all the business I put in his way, during years and years and years. Not the big stuff, of course – he was not up to it; but little things galore. And I used to say to him: There you are, another law-suit for you; try and conduct it better than last time. If I were not such a good friend to you I'd go to So-and-so and have it done quicker and better, but I stick to you, for old times' sake. I often used to pull his leg about it. He was a very witty raconteur, you know, and quick in repartee, and I used to say: If only you were as good in the Law Court as you are in the drawing-room, I might even give you a plum, juggling on the overseas markets, perhaps. And the trouble I took to point out his mistakes to him. Over and over again. Because I am at home in these things; naturally, I have to be. And then this. The arrant nastiness of it.'

He crushed his cigarette and lit a new one.

'It is queer, you know,' he continued. 'But when I look back upon past events and the people who used to be my friends, none of them behaved really well. Not one of them. I cannot understand it.'

He fell silent.

The old lady raised her eyes and looked at him. An old Army joke, beloved by her brother, flitted through her mind. The whole squadron was out of step; only our Jamie wasn't.

'What am I to say?' she answered at last. 'I deeply sympathize with you. Don't you think, though, possibly, that you occasionally upset people by your frankness? You point out mistakes, you correct. You mentioned it yourself just now. Some people cannot bear it.'

'Ah, bah, nonsense. Why should I not tell them if it is true? And then, how could they ever improve if one did not tell them where they have gone wrong? I cannot see it.'

'Just the same, Oscar,' replied the old lady. 'You should try to relax more and take life and people as they are. For your own sake, believe me. I have known you for some time now and I know your many excellent qualities. If you spared others, you would spare yourself.'

'I don't agree with you,' said Oscar Ritter. 'We each have the philosophy which suits us. You are a *grande dame*; you were born like this and you took life as you found it because it was a pleasant life. But what about myself? If I had been content with my circumstances and lived my life as I found it, I would still stand behind the counter and wrap up your sweets for you. Not even that. Because my father's shop was not up to much. I am afraid even Emma might have turned up her nose at it.'

She smiled. 'I am glad to see that you are more yourself again. What do you say? Shall we have some coffee now?'

He closed his eyes and took a deep breath. 'I should like it very much. You are very kind and very understanding. And, of course, what I just told you is strictly *entre nous*. I shall not even tell Margot; it would upset her. I shall wait till she is better again.'

'I should not tell her at all, Oscar. I hid the letter for you because I guessed by the stamp that it was – from that person. I had no idea that Margot knows as much as she does. It amazes me, to be quite frank. You said something during your story – I did not want to interrupt you at the time. To the effect that you mentioned that person to Margot. It was about the household linen, if I am not mistaken.'

'You are quite right.'

'I am an old woman, Oscar. And only fit to sit about and make comments. Many of the new ideas are better than the old ones, I grant you this. My generation is being accused nowadays for the hypocrisy with which we conducted our lives. But it was not all cant, believe me. A lot of what is called morals is only good sense. I don't like this new fashion of facing facts and being frank. It seems to me that honesty is often a cloak for brutality and bad temper. I suppose I am being old-fashioned, but I think you are

203

making a mistake by discussing your past liaisons with Margot. I cannot see any good arising from it.'

'Why not? She can't possibly mind. She knows it is all over and done with. If it was not, I would not tell her.'

'Probably,' replied the old lady. 'Yet there is such a thing as being jealous of the past. The dead are always with us. Feelings are not reasonable, Oscar.'

'But they should be. This is ridiculous. And besides, if I have a wife whom I love and trust, she must be able to understand everything about me. I would not have it otherwise. What is the good of having a wife, if she does not share everything? I must be able to unburden myself. If two people live together, they must help each other. She must share all my worries. If I did not love her so much, I would not expect it from her.'

'It's all very praiseworthy, I'm sure,' replied the old lady. 'Have it your own way. I hope sincerely that you are right. I am very sorry for you, Oscar. More than I can say.'

'Thank you,' he replied. 'The whole affair is most unpleasant. I don't know how long it will take me to get over it.'

'Yes. That. But I was not thinking about it just now. Do you think you could go and find Emma? If she makes the coffee herself, so much the better; it is not my cook's strongest point. And afterwards, if you want to retire, I shall understand. I don't think that you will be in the mood to hear about the fair.'

As he went out, she closed the book which had lain open on her lap, and while placing it on the table, she picked up a singed moth from the base of the lamp.

'Poor devil,' she said and dropped it on the floor.

CHAPTER 21

THE NEXT day brought unsettled weather, wind and swift-moving clouds. Only from time to time the sun broke through and a few ragged patches of azure were revealed in the sky.

It was half past ten in the morning. Mrs. Birk-Borovec sat in front of her dressing-table. She was fully dressed beneath the peignoir of flowered silk which was draped over her shoulders. With her open white hair, rolling in thick waves over her back, her wide and commanding forehead and the majestic double chin above the pearl-grey satin ribbon round her throat, she looked like one of those monumental marble busts of the baroque period which combine the curled and periwigged worldliness of their time with an Olympian detachment.

Standing slightly behind her, a maid holding several hair pins between her lips was rummaging in one of the half-open drawers.

They heard a drumming on the door.

'Come in, Tony,' said the old lady. In the glass she saw Mr. Birk entering and heard the clatter of his boots behind her.

Then, as he sat down on the bed, she could only see the reflection of his knees encased in whipcord breeches and one of his hands rubbing his legs.

'I had a stiff half-hour, Ida. So I thought I'd look in,' he informed her. 'What do you think of the weather? I think the good spell is over for good. I don't care one way or the other. The main lot of the harvest is in, and the beet – that comes later on and can take care of itself. If it rains a lot, let it. The beet will be muddy and weigh more. I won't quarrel with the Almighty; I have no bones to pick with him. Still, if I was a proper farmer, I'd grumble my head off all the time. Oscar was quite right about what he said this morning. Phew.'

'So you had your talk with him and the agent?' asked the old lady. She turned her head to one side, as the maid divided her hair into several strands and began to twist them into a plait. 'I can hold the pins and pass them to you,' she said to the maid.

'No, thank you, madam; I can manage.'

'First a *tête-à-tête* with Oscar,' said Mr. Birk. 'Then a triangle, as the French would call it, with the agent being the third. But not so amusing, Ida. Or perhaps it was, but I could not see the joke. Then I got out of it and they are still at it, for all I know. I suppose Holub will come out alive. He is a big strong man, eh, Ida?'

For a while there was no other sound but the clatter of the combs on the table, the swish of hair as it was brushed and the heavy breathing of the maid.

'I thought things were quite good,' continued Mr. Birk. 'But apparently they aren't. Not a hope yet of getting to the end of the mortgage. And then, checking the accounts, you should have seen Oscar. Of course, I have not got much of a brain outside the stables, never said I had. But before I had even started, he was down at the end of a column and had worked out percentages and heaven knows what. The agent is quite a good chap, really, so long as he does not start with his development piffle, and as I said to him, you don't want to canter before you can trot, and just forget it for a moment. Our parents had no electricity either and lived quite happily without it. As I said, he's quite sound, but by the time I left the books looked more like salad than anything else, and what they look like now, I don't want to know.'

'Do you want a glass of brandy, Tony?'

'No, thank you; I want at least three.'

At a glance and a nod from her mistress, the maid hurried out of the room.

'You know, Ida,' said Mr. Birk and crossed his legs with a savage jerk, 'it's nothing to worry about as things stand, and I don't know how we managed to rub along during the past few years, and I can't add up a column of figures properly but I can tell you this. If it wasn't for Oscar's backing, we'd be out of house and home and good-bye to Kirna.'

She turned round slowly and faced him. 'I should like your opinion, Tony, on something which has just passed my mind. Only an idle fancy, of course. What is your impression about Oscar's attitude to Kirna? I don't mean to us as a family, but to the estate? Is he interested in it for its own sake? Or do you feel that he puts his money into it only because of Margot.'

'There you've got me.' He rubbed his knee thoughtfully. 'He is terribly keen, of course, as sharp as a knife and ten questions before you can answer one. But this does not mean anything with him. I mean, he's never satisfied until he's got all the assets and debits lined up and put in the balance; that's the way he is made and I suppose his mother thought he was a lovely kid. But beyond that. Sometimes you cannot even tell with a horse when the kick is coming.'

'But what is your own feeling about it, Tony?'

'I should say he is bored with Kirna, Ida. For one thing, estate and crops are not his line. He likes things to move fast, up and down, the way it goes on the Stock Exchange. Once you have planted your beet you cannot juggle with it and have to sit on your bottom and wait. And besides, Kirna is not in the pink, as I told you, and it's not a pleasure to have it on your hands, for him, that is. So there you are. Now, what's this about your idle fancy? You are a bit too old for daydreaming, eh, Ida? What do you say?'

'I am worried, Tony. I don't like it at all. I have nothing to go on by—— Come in.'

The brandy was brought and placed on the washstand.

'I see you have brought two glasses,' said the old lady. 'So I will have a drop myself. When you have poured out, Ruzena, you can leave us and I shall call you when I am ready. Half a glass for me, please. Thank you.'

When they were alone, Mr. Birk put his empty glass on the bedside table next to the clock, which he regarded with an affectionate glance. Then he turned to his sister.

'Go on, Ida, let's have it. The sooner it's over, the better.'

'I don't like it, Tony, as I told you – the whole set-up. Margot and Oscar.'

'Neither do I, Ida, but what about it? You have not married him and I haven't.'

208

'But Margot has, Tony. And she has swallowed more than she can chew, to put it crudely. There is trouble ahead, sooner or later. I am afraid it will be sooner.'

'But hang it all, Ida. Wait till I get myself more brandy. It will grease my tongue. There. As I said, what's the fuss about? I can't see it, so help me God. She has got everything she wants – a roof over her head and clothes and frills and heaven knows what besides.'

'True, Tony. And heaven knows what besides. Oscar is not an easy person to live with.'

''Course he isn't, Ida. If he stayed here for a long time, I'd wring his neck or kick him down the back stairs, and if I did not, then Emma would, or Prochazka. I'd help him to a good long sleep, make no mistake about it. But damn it all, he keeps Margot like a queen and he dotes on her. Anybody can see it in five minutes, just the way he looks at her.'

'Yes, Tony. That is the trouble. If he was not so fond of her, it would be easier for her. He makes too many demands on Margot. I had a talk with him yesterday and it frightened me. What he calls love is an excuse for letting himself go, and his idea of marriage is one long whine and moan, with the wife being there for comfort and solace. I can understand it, but Margot is the wrong woman for him. For one thing, she is much too young. And altogether it is hopeless. He forces her into a role for which she is not suited. No good will come out of it, Tony.'

'I know what you mean, Ida. Don't I know it. He expects the ox to calve. And when he does not, he reproaches the ox for being inconsiderate. That's the worst of these rich chaps, Ida. They are too used to getting everything.'

'Exactly, Tony. And he does not see that he is unreasonable and drives her on and on. He puts pressure on her the whole time; his love for her and his bad state of health.'

Mr. Birk rose and went to the washstand. He filled his glass and drained it in two gulps.

'It's no use beating about the bush, Ida. You always talk so nicely and wrap up everything in tissue-paper and pink ribbons. The way I see it, the fellow is a blackguard. Very polite blackmail, all delicate emotions and sighs, but blackmail nevertheless. I have known it all along, Ida. When he wants something, he goes for it, and when he can't get it, he puts the heels in and uses the whip.'

He filled his glass again and took it to the bed, where he sat down.

'He told me a lot about himself last night, Tony,' said the old lady and folded her hands in her lap. 'A very unsavoury affair which has happened to him. Outright blackmail, no doubt about it. Naturally, he was very upset. One of his best friends, Tony. He is bewildered and does not understand. I am very sorry for him.'

'I am not,' replied Mr. Birk. 'Does not get you anywhere. He got a drop of his own medicine, by the looks of it. And talking about him does not get us anywhere either. I have had my bellyful of Oscar this morning. What are you worried about? Margot is getting up today and in a day or two they will be gone and that will be the end of it. Prince Podolsky sends his regards. I ran into him at the fair last night. Enquired about Margot *très tendrement*. Just as well Oscar was not with us.'

'That's nothing, Tony. For one thing, Margot turns

people's heads, but beyond that she does not go. She is not really interested. Besides, Oscar is the last man on earth to be jealous. He thinks he is such a good catch for a woman that no woman would ever look at anybody else.'

'Thank God for that, Ida. There you are. So long as Margot does not run away with somebody – and you say she won't – everything is in clover. She'll settle down and get used to it. You can get used to anything.'

The old lady shook her head. 'Not always, Tony. There are things one never forgives and never forgets. But let it go.'

'Very well. Now I'll tell you something funny I have been wanting to tell you all along. Last night, when I was chatting with the Prince, the young postmaster from Celakovice came up to us – staggered up to us, I should say. Drunk isn't the word for it. He recognized us and button-holed the Prince and told him that now that we've got the Republic and democracy, we were all equal and something to that effect. I suppose he had been reading the newspapers. We are all equal now, he said, and to me you are no more Prince Podolsky. Plain Mr. Podolsky, from now on. I am Mr. Fiala and you are Mr. Podolsky. You, mister. And not sir. So the Prince said, I see what you mean, Fiala. I will address you as you, Mr. Fiala, as I have always done, but you, from now on can say "thou Podolsky" to me. Because there must be some sort of distinction between us.'

Mr. Birk slapped his thigh and chuckled.

The old lady laughed so heartily that tears came into her eyes and she had to wipe her face. 'I can just see it,' she gasped. 'And now, Tony, if you please, call for Ruzena, or I will never get dressed. And leave the brandy here. It will be safer.'

CHAPTER 22

MARGOT CAME down before lunch, looking very pretty and sulky. Her husband was still upstairs, having a brush-up and a wash after his strenuous morning, which had been concluded by an excursion through the farm buildings: 'I don't know why people always exult in the smell of cow-sheds and stables. To me they stink.'

She strayed into the saints' room, where she found Raoul Marek, who looked glumly through an old copy of *Country Life*. He jumped up as she entered.

'I am so glad to see you well again, Mrs. Ritter. Is it completely over? The pains gone?'

She dropped into a chair facing him. She tilted her head slightly and fingered an amethyst brooch which was fastened to the ruffled collar of her lace blouse. Her fair and faintly rosy skin reminded him of the field-grown poppies he had seen on Saturday. He noticed with admiration that she did not freckle.

'Yes, thank you. It's all over now. I still feel a bit weak, of course, but then, as my grandmother says, lying in bed makes one weak. It is all very tiresome. And it is just my luck to get up when the weather has changed.'

She fluttered her eyelids in the direction of the window and then turned her head away with one of her charmingly soft movements.

'Perhaps it's just as well, though,' she added. 'Oscar wants to leave in a day or two and it would break my heart to have to leave with the sun blazing and everything looking its best. Still, I shall hate to go, weather or no weather.'

'But you can always return,' ventured the young man. 'Whenever you feel like it.'

'No,' she answered curtly. 'Oscar can't get away from town. In a month's time they are starting the campaign – why they call it campaign, I shall never know – and that is the busiest time of the year. It has always seemed to me that sugar is a peculiar business. All the year round the factories stand idle and are being cleaned and painted and fitted up to date and then for six weeks in autumn they get the beet in and work like mad. I could never understand how they can make enough profit for the rest of the year. Can you?'

'Not really. But then, I don't know anything about it. Though I quite agree there is something hectic and unnatural about this sudden rush.'

'It's unnatural altogether,' replied Margot and fell into a reverie. After a while she added: 'The sugar, I mean.' Then she smiled with an effort and asked in a changed voice: 'And you, Mr. Marek? How long are you going to stay?'

'I am leaving the day after tomorrow; that will be a Wednesday. I arrived last Wednesday, you know.'

'Oscar wants to leave here on Wednesday, too. I wish we could take you in the car, but I am afraid that is out of the question. We have so much luggage, unfortunately. And then, there is the chauffeur. If Oscar would drive himself, we could have squeezed you in. But Oscar never does. He is too nervy, you know.'

'It is of no importance, Mrs. Ritter. It is only an hour by train.'

They were silent. Margot looked straight ahead of her, playing with her brooch. The young man felt uneasy and resumed his reflections. He would have liked to question her, but felt it to be impossible. He had received a letter from his partner in the morning, which he was at a loss to understand. 'I shall be staying here for another fortnight. The weather is superb. I have news for you, but it will keep till I get back. How are you enjoying your stay with the Birks? If I were you, I should beat a retreat gracefully, dear Raoul. As long as you are my partner, you will not be *persona grata* with that family. I should advise you to hunt for your butterfly elsewhere. Miss B. is not the only rich girl in the world, and after my experience, one finds them in unexpected places.'

'I have had a lovely time here,' he remarked.

'Why don't you stay another week?' asked Margot. 'There will be more people coming out next week-end. A friend of my mother's with her daughter and a sculptor from Vienna. He is a very interesting man, a special friend of Uncle Tony.' She giggled.

'How amazing,' said the young man. 'I would not have thought – although there is more in your uncle than meets the eye.'

She continued to giggle. 'Oh, it's nothing to do with art. It is sheer spite. You know Aunt Louise; she is grandmother's and Uncle Tony's sister and they don't speak. Rita was Aunt Louise's only daughter and she went to Vienna when she was nineteen and studied art. There she met this sculptor and became his mistress and lived with him in sin for twenty years till she died. It was a scandal and a disgrace in the family, as you can imagine. After her death Uncle Tony got in touch with the man and invited him, in order to annoy my aunt, and he has kept it up ever since. He is awfully nice, though. Very big and strong – he has to be – because chiselling is hard work, and very simple. He drinks sour milk all day long and the servants adore him.'

'How remarkable,' said the young man.

'Oscar does not care for him, though,' continued Margot. 'He met him once, while staying here and he wanted to have a proper talk with him, but the sculptor drivelled the whole evening about floor polish and how he kept his studio floors clean and reminisced about the charwomen he had had in his Paris days. It was terribly funny.'

'Oh, quite so. Absolutely.' What a queer lot they were, he thought.

'And then, when he was in his studio in Paris, so to speak, and almost at the point to discuss sculpture, Uncle Tony started about his groom Robinson, and that was the end. Oscar was white with anger. I have to laugh when I remember it.'

Did they ever do anything else, he wondered, except indulge in their family squabbles? They seemed to exist for this sole purpose. That was, he supposed, what one called 'living for one's family'. He suppressed the nervous laughter which rose in his throat. And while his glance wandered over the ceiling, over those dimpled pink arms, and curling toes, those puffed-up cheeks and cherubic pouting lips, those twisted veils and fluttering cloaks, he reflected that if the Birks had no love, they had at least hatred; good strong hatred, nourished during years, something to hold on to and to cherish. And he felt, to his own amazement, slightly envious. Then his thoughts went back to his partner's letter.

Alice's voice was heard outside: 'This is just like her. When it's boiling hot, she sends up hot dishes, and when it's cool, we get a cold platter. Salad. If at least she had asked me. I could weep.'

Then Emma, low and crisp: 'She thought Mr. Oscar would want something light, seeing that after last night he complained it was too heavy for him.'

'She thought, she thought. I am not interested in her thoughts. And Emma, put Mr. Oscar's drops on the table today. This morning at breakfast he forgot to take them and nobody reminded him. He has so much on his mind, he cannot remember everything. You know, he always says, he does not want to be waited upon; he wants to be helped. We must all try and help him, Emma.'

'Yes, madam.'

After this, Alice entered.

'If I were you, Margot, I would go upstairs and see if Oscar has everything he wants. He has had a gruelling morning with the accounts and he has had a bad night and does not feel so good.'

'I have only just come down, mother. He is changing and he will be here in a minute. Did he say anything to you? Ruzena is still about, if he wants anything.'

Alice pressed her lips together. 'You sometimes amaze me, Margot. You know perfectly well that the maids get on his nerves because they kiss his hand and he thinks it's not hygienic. He is quite right, of course.'

'He is always right, mother.'

'I am glad you see it,' replied Alice.

'And he will go on being always right and one day he will see that he is right and alone.'

'What on earth do you mean? I still think you should go upstairs. I am sure Mr. Marek will excuse you, won't you, Mr. Marek?'

Margot got up with a jerk. Her chair scraped over the floor with a squeaking noise. She went out and slammed the door.

'She is sometimes so brusque, Mr. Marek,' remarked Alice. 'For no reason at all. That's youth. I always say to her: You shall see; life will rub off your corners yet. We all meet our Waterloo, Mr. Marek.'

'Quite so. Absolutely.'

'She should be grateful for what she has got. She has everything anybody could wish for. But one is always grateful when it is too late; life has taught me this, and I think you know it as well as I do. That poem, you remember, how does it go?

> Oh love as long as love you can,
> Oh love as long as love will keep;
> The hour will come, the hour will come,
> When by the grave you'll kneel and weep.

We learnt it at school. Did you, too? They have changed the poems nowadays, I believe.'

'It's a deuce of a fine poem, Alice,' shouted Mr. Birk from the door. 'Don't I remember it. Max had to recite it once at school and he had a cold and brought the house down. "Oh nove as nong as nove you can, oh nove as nong as nove win keep." Why, he made history with it. You ask Ida; she'll tell you.'

'You gave me quite a start, Uncle Tony. I did not see you coming. Won't you sit down?'

'No fear. I just thought I would look in. Where is Margot?'

'Upstairs with Oscar.'

'Ah well, I'll tell her later. I have just seen the gardener. He says Oscar should should take a few drops of valerian; it will make him sleep better.'

'How absurd,' replied Alice. 'As though Oscar would want his advice.'

'It's not that exactly, Alice. Don't worry though; I won't pass it on to the gentleman. Because what if it did work? What then? Oscar would never forgive us, hahaha. Now I must trot off. Zuleika Dobson is laming. No good asking you or this individual here what to do. Eh, young Raoul?'

'I am afraid I don't understand horses, Mr. Birk.'

'She is not just a horse, let me tell you. She is an Arab.'

'Oh yes. They are very fiery, aren't they?'

'Fiery my elbow. People always get ideas when they don't know what it's all about. She has got temperament, my boy, but only on the surface. It's like a straw fire. All show and no heat. But she is worldly wise. Knows a thing or two and it isn't all goodness. If I had to sell her, I would settle her hash. Lame her on the other leg as well, and she would walk even. That's the way it's done. My groom Robinson was a marvel at that sort of job. You've got to know how to do it. But this does not get me anywhere now. I've got to get her going again properly. Can't always find a sucker, can I, my boy? Well, so long.'

After the clatter of the boots had faded away, Alice said with a disapproving shake of her head: 'Always the groom Robinson. He was a horrible man, Mr. Marek. An evil influence, I always felt. The expressions he used. In English, of course, so it was not so bad. But still. Uncle Tony says they were nothing to what Lord Kirkwood used. Which is impossible, of course. He only tried to shield Robinson. I did not always understand, yet I knew. One always knows what is wrong and what isn't, don't you think so? And besides, it has never been clear to me why people have to swear. Surely, we can express ourselves in nice and decent words and bad language is so unnecessary. And the amazing thing about it, Mr. Marek, or perhaps it is not so amazing, because it is the way of the world; the longer it is ago, the better groom Robinson becomes, in my uncle's eyes. In a few years' time he will be a saint. I should not be surprised.' She paused and her eyes, disapproving and restless, swept over the uneasy splendour of the ceiling.

Raoul Marek, too, looked up, wondering if a space could be spared among those wriggling bodies and windswept garments.

'I could easily imagine it,' he replied with a tentative smile. 'Mr. Birk is so wholehearted in his thoughts and convictions. I think he is quite capable of adding Robinson's picture to the rest up there.'

'He is capable of anything, Mr. Marek. Don't I know it. Of course, it is inherited, although it does not make it any better. There is a streak of grandeur in the family. Have you seen the library? In the Gothic wing?'

'Giving on to the terrace, at the end where the garden-room lies? I saw it. I thought it was a chapel; it looks so religious somehow.'

'That's because of the oriel windows. My grandfather built it. Nobody knows why. It is only one room, completely round inside and fitted up with shelves for books. It has long blue velvet curtains, all moth-eaten and mildewed, and imitation Gothic chairs with carved trefoils, sham baronial; very bad taste, I must say, although it was my own grandfather. He never used the room, nor did anybody else. He was not the reading kind. Every year when grandfather had his birthday, Uncle Karel – that was Louise's husband, you know – used to say, what shall we give the old man as a present? Not a book, because he has got one already. Mind you, one can go to the other extreme too, with reading. Uncle Gustav did. He fell in the war. He would read the whole time, most unhealthy in my opinion. One day, when he was in barracks, he started on a book and did not like it and threw it out of the window. Some time later the Colonel passed, picked it up from the mud and said to his aide: That's Lieutenant Birk's book; see that he gets it. How can you tell, sir? Because, said the Colonel, Birk is the only man in my Company who reads. Of course, Uncle Gustav was a bit eccentric. I am very broadminded though; I know that taste varies, and I think reading is all right so long as it does not interfere with other things. But I always find, in the long run, people are apt to neglect their work because of their hobbies and someone else has to do the work for them. I have always had a sense of duty, thank God.'

CHAPTER 23

LUNCH WAS not a cheerful meal, it seemed to Raoul Marek. He was still digesting the contents of the letter, and after having repeatedly told himself during the last few hours that he was not welcome with his hosts, he achieved to work himself up into a feeling of guilt, although he had not an inkling about what he should feel guilty. He observed the others and their attitude to him, and he saw that Oscar Ritter and Margot were bad-tempered. Also, that Mr. Ritter avoided addressing him and avoided even his glance. Mr. Birk prattled on as usual, but this did not mean that he was well disposed; there was no telling. On the other hand, why should the Ritters not be bad-tempered; there was no reason why he should be the cause of it. It was probably a coincidence. Thus he argued with himself and sank more deeply into his gloom.

'That head gardener of yours is a fool,' remarked Oscar Ritter to the old lady. 'We met him during our tour today. He showed us the cactus in the glasshouse, how it grows up to the ceiling and then bends at an angle and grows right along beneath the roof, because it cannot stop growing. He is so in love with it that he wants to have the glasshouse pulled down and enlarged. Frittering away his job on this idiotic plant and in the rest of the place he grows geraniums and lobelias which are no good to anybody. And when I say anything, he tells me that they were old Mr. Birk's favourite flowers and how pleased he would be if he could see the cactus today. It's no use running an estate with people who are fifty years behind their time.'

His speech was received in silence.

The salad was brought in, surrounded by the flora which blooms only in the kitchen. There were red roses formed of lobster claws and deep red ones of beetroot, tightly rolled rosebuds of smoked salmon and white and green ones of parsley butter, flowers of hard-boiled egg and small bundles of asparagus tips and tomatoes dotted with mayonnaise which looked like toadstools.

'Well, Oscar,' said Mr. Birk. 'Inspection tours are never any good. You might have saved your temper. If you announce yourself in advance, it's a put-up job and conceals the true state of things, and if you see it in the raw you are not pleased. And in the end you get wise to the make-believe, too. I feel about it like old General Jaroschy. When he inspected the garrison in Brandys, he came to the lavatories and shouted: What's the lavatory paper for? And when nobody answered he said: I'll tell you; it's for eyewash. Leave the gardener to himself. He's done his job for donkey's years.'

'Exactly. That's the trouble.'

Then came cutlets fried in breadcrumbs.

'I saw the cactus yesterday,' said Raoul Marek to Bettine.

'I was very impressed. Does it ever flower?'

'No. All the strength goes into growing. At least, that's what the gardener says. Did he show you the scar?'

'No.'

'That is where one of the dogs from Semtin bit a chunk out of it. The dog was sick afterwards and the cactus never grew on this spot. Bypassed it, so to speak and grew all around it. The dog was sick in the dining-room and Uncle Tony sent the carpet to Semtin with the dog, when the boys went back home. Aunt Mila sent us another carpet, but she did not speak for two years. The carpet was not spoiled at all, mind you. It was rotten anyhow, but Uncle Tony did it as a gesture. When Aunt Mila has her birthday, he sends her a few cacti every year; that's ten years ago now and he still keeps it up. She puts them in the cellar; she says she has no room for them upstairs. And so it goes on.'

She helped herself to French beans.

The young man followed suit. 'But how does one do it? I mean, how do you do it, when you don't speak? Does it mean that when your Aunt Mila is cross with Mr. Birk, their families don't speak either?'

'That depends,' replied Bettine, 'how serious it is. With Aunt Mila it was strictly between her and Uncle Tony. We went there all the time and the boys came here. But with Aunt Louise, for instance, it is more widespread. And then I remember Uncle Max – that is Mila's husband – crossed swords with Uncle Gustav, the one who fell in the war. It was something about a silly post card Gustav had sent him from Switzerland, with a funny dog on it, because Max is so keen on dogs. Then – I recall it very well, I was quite small at the time but it was rather vivid – Uncle Gustav came to visit his brother in Semtin and the boys – they were children, too – crawled up to him on all fours and said vow, vow and bit him. Then Gustav was cross and accused Max of having trained the boys to do it. Uncle Max was offended and would not speak, and when mama heard about it, she said that if Max was silly enough not to speak then he was not worth being spoken to either. So she and Uncle Gustav kept it up for years with Max. That is why I say it always depends.'

The young man chewed and swallowed and then enquired: 'Did it ever happen that everybody was on good terms with all the others?'

Bettine looked thoughtful. 'Not as far as I can remember. You should ask mama; she might tell you. It is possible that when the grandparents were still alive things went a bit smoother.'

She finished slowly what was on her plate.

Eclairs were served, filled with a cream of Gruyère cheese and dusted with red pepper.

'Our family is a bit spiteful,' continued Bettine. 'Sometimes they carry it very far. A great-aunt of mine, a cousin of mama's, had a claim on a stretch of land on the estate. She was in the right and she was not; you know how these things go. You come up against it everyday in your office, don't you? She did not want to go to court, because she was not well off and did not want to risk the costs. She threatened that she would commit suicide if my family did not give in. They did not give in and she killed herself. She left a letter, blaming us for it. She was determined to have the last word, you see.'

'Good Lord!'

Bettine smiled. 'We are really very moderate, when you come to think of it. But imagine if we had lived in the times of the Borgias.'

There came an almond pudding with chocolate sauce. The young man took a large helping. He felt relieved. At any rate, Bettine bore him no grudge. She was as friendly as ever. So was Alice. He realized that the relating of anecdotes by the Birks about the Birks was a favour, only bestowed upon outsiders who were well thought of. He cursed Robert Kramar. He hated hinting and secretiveness. Very likely it would boil down to nothing at all. Or perhaps not. The wording of the letter indicated something definite. Harrowed by doubt, he stopped eating and drew furrows through the pudding on his plate, which he deftly flooded with chocolate sauce. What a pretty little landscape it looked, ragged and jagged and honeycombed by a river.

'There,' said Bettine and she planted a plume of parsley which had dropped on the cloth into the highest ridge.

'I don't know if I approve of it,' said the young man. 'This is a mountainous place. Do you think it would have trees?'

A rustle by his elbow made him stop.

'Have you finished, sir?' murmured Emma's voice behind him.

CHAPTER 24

IT WAS three o'clock in the afternoon. The kitchen smelled of hot raspberry jam and wax polish. A yellow flypaper, thickly dotted with dead flies, hung from a lamp like a strip of leopard skin. The shelves and tables were covered with scalloped linen embroidered in blue cross stitch and lined with white and blue striped jars. The blue and white checked curtains in front of the tightly shut double windows revealed a few pots with chive and four hens moving feebly in the narrow space between the panes. The fire in the coal range crackled faintly and transformed this place, so cosy in winter, into an inferno during the hot season.

The agent's wife stood behind a table and rubbed flour through a sieve on to a board. She was a tall and fragile woman with a straight and graceful bearing. Her dark brown hair fell over her forehead in a fringe which had been fashionable in her girlhood; she curled it daily with a hot iron. Her white face was small and beautiful, shaped with the regularity of a statue. Yet its beauty was not that of the stern marble, but of the gentler alabaster. She wore a brown dress with a frill round the neck and an apron of printed cotton. A tap on the window made her look up, and with a smile she nodded her head at Margot, who stood outside with her face pressed against the glass. She wiped her hands on the apron and unlatched the kitchen door. Then she wiped her hands again.

Margot came in, laughing and dangling her bag on her wrist. 'Mrs. Holub,' she said and stood still. The agent's wife put both arms round her shoulders and for a second they looked into each other's eyes with the smile gone from their faces.

'It's lovely to see you again,' said Margot. 'I wanted to come sooner, but I did not have a chance.'

'I thought so.'

'And are you at it again? It's only three and you are already cooking.'

'Yes, that's the way it is,' said the older woman. 'It takes longer to make than to eat it. Would you like some coffee?'

'Yes, please. I need it. I had so much to eat for lunch that I nearly fell asleep afterwards. But finish your do first. What is it? Dumplings?'

'Yes. Dumplings. He won't eat anything else. Sometimes rice or noodles, but never a potato with the meat.'

Margot sat down on the bench which was fixed along the narrow side of the range and watched the agent's wife, who finished sieving the flour, then swept it into a bowl, broke two eggs in it, poured milk in, sprinkled salt, and began to beat the dough with a wooden spoon.

'I brought you a present from Rome.'

'Dear me. You should not have bothered. I am sure you had other people to remember. Madam your mother and all the family. Fancy that you thought of me.'

'Of course I did. I'll put it on for you, may I? You have got floury hands.'

She produced from a wrapping of tissue-paper a golden chain with a rose carved out of a large pink coral.

'It's a replica of the golden rose of the Pope, Mrs. Holub, and it has been blessed by him.'

'Dear me. I don't think I can accept it, Miss Margot; it is too valuable. It is not fitting that you should give me anything so precious. And I am sure Mr. Ritter is not pleased if you spend his money like this on people like me.'

'Oh, don't be silly,' said Margot. 'It's nothing grand, not as good as you deserve. And besides, I might just as well spend his money while I have still got it. If you don't accept it, I shall be offended.'

'Well, in that case. But I don't know how to thank you.'

Brought up in a generation when it was not polite to accept anything unless pressed to do so repeatedly, and lacking all conceit, the agent's wife suffered Margot to fasten the trinket after several further protestations.

'Can I grind the coffee?' asked Margot. 'I know where it is.'

And without waiting she took the coffee-mill from the shelf, sat down on the bench and began to turn the handle.

'You have grown thinner,' said Mrs. Holub and raised her voice above the grating sound issuing from the mill. 'And you have lost colour. It suits you; it gives you more finesse, but it should not be. I suppose it's from your illness. You can't shake off an illness in a minute. I was told you had bad pains.'

Mrs. Holub always used the formula 'I was told'. Its impersonality suited her. In her isolation, living, as she did, in a social no-man's-land, above the maids and beneath the masters, she could not indulge in gossip as freely as other women can. It was this position between the servants' hall and the drawing-room, shared by governesses and paid companions all over the world, which had sharpened her sense of what was fitting and increased her natural shyness. She was one of those natures who lack aggressiveness and are affectionate, without having passion. Being too soft to hold her own, her marriage had subdued her into a constant state of repressed sadness. Had she been born in circumstances similar to those of the Birks, she would have shrunk from men and life like Bettine and assumed the cool inaccessibility which is the armour of the helpless.

Margot made a face. 'Oh, that. It wasn't anything. But I had a rest. Not long enough, but still. I think there is nothing like peace and quietness, don't you? It helps you to sort yourself out. I never felt like this before. I am getting old, I suppose.' She giggled and turned the handle vigorously.

The agent's wife put fried bread cubes into the bowl, stirred and dipped the dough on to the floured board. Then she soaked a clean cloth in water, wrung it out and spread melted butter on it with a feather brush.

The grinding stopped. 'I am through with it,' said Margot and rested her arm on her knee. 'Completely through. Shall I put the water on?'

'No, thank you. Just go into the parlour and sit down. I'll be with you in a minute. I don't know what anybody would say, seeing me entertaining you in the kitchen. I am

ashamed of myself.' With these words, Mrs. Holub placed
the dough on the cloth, shaped it into a sausage, wrapped it
up and tied both ends with string.

Margot stepped into the parlour and sat down in a chair by
the tile stove. The tiles, glazed and brown and with a round
dip in the middle, seemed to look at her with staring eyes.
The room, curtained with green and bobble-fringed plush,
lay in a greenish twilight, impervious to the seasons and the
weather. She closed her eyes and remained motionless, with
her hands clenched into fists, until the agent's wife entered.

She turned her head. 'It's nice to sit on a soft easy chair
again. Uncle Tony always says you've got the only comfortable chairs in the place. We haven't got one like it in the
castle.'

'He likes to have his little jokes. He says the same to me.
He has got a way with him to put people at their ease. A
real gentleman.'

'I suppose he is, Mrs. Holub.'

'Of course he is.' She put the coffee-tray on a small table
and placed it in front of the young girl.

'Always the same to everybody. And if he were in rags
and down and out, which heaven forbid, he would still be
the same with people.'

She sat down and busied herself with the cups and plates.
'I have not got anything special for you, Miss Margot. Just
our ordinary fare. If I had known you would be coming——'

'Oh nonsense. It looks lovely. And your coffee is always
better than ours. And besides, I did not know till the last
minute myself. Oscar went to lie down after lunch. He is
worn out. As usual.'

'He had a busy morning, I was told.'

Margot stirred her cup moodily. 'Yes. Don't I know it. He never lets us forget when he has been busy. Why, I should like to know. If it is too much for him, he should not do it and if he decides to do it, then it was his own free will and there is no need to squeal about it afterwards. But I am no longer interested to know why and why not. As the French say, *il ne faut pas tâcher de comprendre.*' She gave a little laugh.

'Marriage is give and take, Miss Margot. More coffee?'

'Yes, thank you. But it's no good. Not with me, in any case. There is something wrong if one does all the giving and the other all the taking. And besides, there should be no need for give and take. That is, in a perfect marriage.'

The agent's wife looked at her. With her brown melancholy eyes, her gracefully bent body and the gentle tilt of her white face, she made one think of the sedge and the willows, the white-flowering bindweed and the marsh grass which fledge the River Elbe.

'Well,' she said, 'of course, I have not been about much and mixed in society the way you do, Miss Margot. I have not come across the perfect marriage. But then, I am nobody to lay down the law.'

They remained silent. The place was still and despite the heat it held the chill which emanates from shut up and rarely used rooms. There were no living plants. On a bamboo stand in the corner stood a vase with immortellas and a jar filled with the papery moons of honesty. A bouquet of peacock plumes embellished the space between the windows. A yellow shell, tiger spotted with black, lay on a wall

231

bracket and above it hung a framed picture with a spray of flowers composed of tiny coloured feathers.

Margot put her cup down. 'Mrs. Holub, I am going to leave Oscar. Don't say anything. I have not told anybody yet.'

'You can't. You are not well, Margot. Miss Margot. It's the heat. I thought you looked fagged out as soon as you came in.'

'I am fagged out because I never get a rest. He has been nagging since the first day. I can't stand it any more. And I won't stand it any more. If this is marriage, I don't like it.' She tossed her head and laughed.

'There you go. Laughing. I knew it was only a joke. There. You gave me quite a start, nevertheless. But you should not say such things. Not even in fun.'

'Can I smoke, Mrs. Holub?' Margot lit a cigarette. She leaned back and blew a few curls of smoke. 'It's no good. I cannot do it. The boys from Semtin can blow wonderful rings. I wish I knew the trick,' and lightly, without changing her voice: 'I did not joke, Mrs. Holub. I meant it. I have not had it out with Oscar yet and I cannot tell anybody of the family. Not till I have done it.'

The agent's wife slid to the edge of her chair and bent forward, sad and swaying.

'Miss Margot,' she said, 'I entreat you.' And she wrung her hands for a moment. 'And you should not be sitting here and telling me all about it. If madam your mother knew, I would not dare to look her in the face.'

'Never mind her. Madam my mother will boil up and then she will simmer down again. That is, to a point. She will never simmer down completely. She will have the time of her life, throwing it into my face every time there is an opportunity for it. For ever and ever, amen.'

'Don't say any more, Miss Margot. You are worried and you are trying to laugh it off. But she loves you. They all do. It makes me ill to think of it. If you only had not told me. I've got it on my conscience now.'

'I am sorry. I had to tell somebody. I had to break my heart to you before I face the music. Besides, it won't be so terrible. Bettine won't care. And my grandmother – she will know it all before I open my mouth. It's peculiar; she does not talk and she does not draw you out. She sits all day long on the settee and hardly looks up. And yet, she has got it all at her fingertips. I don't know how she does it.' She laughed and shrugged her shoulders.

'If only you had not told me. The upset. And the scandal of it. We have not been here long, Miss Margot, but I was told what you were like as a little girl and what your mother was like and the old lady. I feel as though I had been with the family all my life. And there never was anything like it before. Never. They will feel it worse than if you were dead.'

'Come, come. It happens every day. You see a divorce every time you open a paper.'

'Ah yes,' replied Mrs. Holub. 'There is much more of it than there used to be. That's all right for them, for the others. But not for you, Miss Margot. With your position and everything.'

'I can't help it. If I am in disgrace, *tant pis*. The boys will still come over, and if Marketa wants to cut me, she can. She could never stand me. She is older than I am and I have been married for a year and she is not even engaged yet. It will give her something to talk about. I can just hear her: Very unfortunate, and yet I cannot help feeling . . . Whenever I go to my dressmaker's in Prague I meet her, and it's always: Only a little dress, only a teeny-weeny nothing. I am sick of the sight of her.'

'There you go working yourself up and all for nothing. Nobody knows yet and I am like the grave, and perhaps you will go home and think it over and go on as though nothing had happened and nobody will know any different.'

'It's too late for that, Mrs. Holub. I have done it so often. I have done it every day. I clenched my teeth and closed my eyes and thought I must take it like medicine. But I have come to the end of my tether. When I am by myself, it is not so bad, but as soon as he is with me, I feel like screaming the whole time. I could hit him. And it is such a terrible effort to conceal it. And yet, I am not savage, you know. I have never felt like this before.'

'I know, Miss Margot. You have got a soft heart.'

'No, I haven't. That's the worst of it.' She lit another cigarette. 'My heart – that is nothing. I am as cool as a cucumber. I knew what I was doing when I married him. He was rich and important and I did not love him and my heart never hurt because of it. It is my nerves, not my heart. He tramples on my nerves.'

The agent's wife looked down on the floor and nodded her head several times.

'I came down here to have a bit of peace and to sort myself out. I thought if I had a few days without him, I could pull myself together again. Or perhaps not. I don't know what I thought, really. Then he came down here straight away when he heard that I was ill – I did not think he would, but he did. And he was at me again from the first minute. And then this, last night – to expect me to sympathize over this. It was the limit. And yet he is such a model husband. It makes it worse. If only he would drink or gamble and leave me alone. Or have other women and not tell me. It's funny, he looks down his nose at the boys because he thinks they are rotters, but my God. I am sick of his loyalty and his sincerity and his sitting in judgment of other people and trying to be fair and laying down the law about everything and nagging and criticizing, as though the other person could never be in the right.'

She drew a deep and trembling breath. 'I can't even weep about it. I feel so bitter that it is choking me.'

She looked in front of her and laughed. 'He does not like the saints because they were not hygienic, but deep down inside him he thinks he is a saint himself.'

'The Christian humility,' said the agent's wife. 'You can't get away from what we learned at school. But the scandal of it, Miss Margot. And you won't be living like you used to now. I was told you got an ermine coat. Have you thought of it?'

'Of course I have. That's nothing. I like it when I have it, but it does not break my heart to go without it. I can go without luxuries.'

She leaned back and contemplated the smoke of her cigarette. The agent's wife looked at her, doubtful and polite. She did not know that the young girl had spoken the truth. She had never come across the frugality which surrounds the childhood of the very rich. She had never seen the black wax-cloth and the linoleum, the white dimity and the cheap prints, the Spartan suppers of boiled egg and milk pudding day in day out. She had never seen those frocks and pinafores which are always made too large, so as to allow for growing, those garments mended to the utmost. She had never been under the reign of those coveted governesses, who, after serving in royal households, spread their austerity in other houses who can afford them, and she did not realize that they stand for getting up at six o'clock and a cold shower, only three presents at Christmas and chocolate boxes locked away, if they ever reach the nursery. And it had never occurred to her that this rigid discipline, coupled with the knowledge that everything will be available in adult life, kills the craving for all which is beyond reach.

'Well,' said Margot, 'here goes. I had better go back into the lions' den. It is so beautifully peaceful here. I wish I could stay for ever.'

'Think of what I said, Miss Margot. Think it over. Once it's done, it will be too late to go back on it. You know I am as silent as the grave. Remember me to the ladies. What will they be feeling? I dare not think of it.'

And she conducted the young girl from the green twilight into the blue and white inferno, wiped her hands on the apron and shook her head repeatedly.

Margot stepped out of the door and heard the click of the latch as it was shut behind her.

The sun was hidden by a sheet of dirty white clouds; the air was hot and torpid, heavy with dust and smells. The short, sanded path lay bordered by the yellow and purple of camomile and thyme and on either side of it grew mignonette and lavender, grey and wilted. A hedge of blackthorn and juniper drooping over the dirty palisade hid the castle from her view, and in its shade grew a mass of nettles, the only streak of juicy green in sight. For the first time in her life she had taken a decision and for the first time she felt alone. With a frown she walked across to the gate and kicked it open with her foot.

CHAPTER 25

'THE WHOLE thing is utterly ridiculous. She does not know her own mind. Besides, she cannot just follow every whim that comes into her head. She is under age, in any case.'

'If she was old enough to be married, she is old enough to know whether she likes it or not. It's only logical.'

'Oh, for heaven's sake, Bettine, stop being so clever-clever. I have gone through life without logic, thank you very much. You don't impress me with your high-faluting words.'

Alice, with a red spot on each cheek, faced her sister across the round table in the drawing-room. Her eyes, with the pupils dilated by anger, looked darker and more wide open than usual.

'Why. If only I knew why,' she said in a lower tone. 'Mama,' she said suddenly. It sounded like a clarion call. 'Do you think that Margot – may Heaven forgive me for thinking of it, and a daughter of mine too, but then, on the other hand, she is her father's daughter as well and blood is thicker than water, I don't think I have to tell you this, do you then——'

'You mean has she got a lover,' said Bettine crisply and turned to the window.

The old lady looked up from her game of patience and glanced at her daughters. Then she lowered her head again, her face was hidden in shadow and only her hair gleamed snowy in the light, framed by the black and golden sphinx behind her.

'That is not what I meant to say,' replied Alice with a hurt voice. 'I only meant, do you think there is another man, mama.'

'I am sure there is not,' said the old lady. Her voice was low and tired. 'Unfortunately not,' she continued, 'there is nothing like a light affair to keep a marriage going. For one thing, it makes the wife happy and contented and secondly it gives her a feeling of guilt and makes her behave specially well to her husband. No, Alice, you will have to look elsewhere.'

'But what else is there? What can there be? And if you know something, mama, then surely it is your duty to tell me.'

'I don't know any more than you do, Alice. They just don't get on.'

'It is as plain as daylight,' said Bettine.

'Oh stop being so knowing, Bettine. You are driving me mad with your superior attitudes.'

'And you are more thick-skinned than I ever thought you were, Alice.'

'Ha. I am not surprised. When all goes well, you never say a word beyond what is necessary, but when there is trouble you go out of your way to gloat. If you understand it as well as all that, why did you not prevent it happening? Why did you never speak up?'

'If you cannot even see that your own daughter is unhappy then it is no use talking.'

'She is not unhappy, let me tell you. She only imagines herself to be.'

'It amounts to the same.'

'Superior again. What right have you got to talk about this sort of thing? I think I have gone through slightly more in life than you have, if you will allow me to say so. Mama. What do you think is going to happen now? If only they made it up and went back to Prague. I would like to see Oscar, but perhaps it is better not to. The way he shut himself up in his room and did not come down to dinner. I don't know what Mr. Marek thought. If only it had not happened here. Oscar might think we encouraged her or something. I should not be at all surprised. I would not blame him. What can you expect when your own sister turns against you.'

'She won't go back with him, Alice,' said the old lady. 'It is the end. I don't know what the quarrel was all about, but I do know that she has made up her mind. It's no good, Alice. You must accept it.'

'But that is impossible, mama. After all – a quarrel, that is nothing. One does not separate after a row. I don't understand you, I must say. The whole thing can't be taken seriously.'

'It is not how we take it. It is how Margot takes it.'

'There is somebody coming,' said Bettine.

Mr. Birk trampled into the room and threw himself on the settee next to the old lady.

'It's no good huddling about like frightened hens,' he

exclaimed. 'Take Margot, take Oscar, make them shake hands, and if they don't, knock their heads together.'

'It is not as simple as that, Uncle Tony,' replied Bettine.

'Nonsense. She will sleep it over and tomorrow she'll be sorry and come round. She is just playing about. Tucked in at dinner and did not even shed a tear. Get away.'

'She has had enough, Tony,' said the old lady. She swept the cards together and put them in the case. 'It was bound to come.'

'Fiddlesticks. We can't have that sort of thing. Just think what Louise will say, when she hears of it. She will be as pleased as punch. No, we can't have it.'

'There is nothing to do about it, Tony.'

'Of course there is. I suppose she was getting bored. I will have a talk with Oscar tomorrow. See that he takes her out more. And give her an interest. A hobby or something. Make her take up Spanish or needle work or charity. What do you say, Ida?'

'Have you ever seen it work, Tony?'

'No.'

He moved his legs and scratched his head. He got up. 'Well, think no more about it. It's eleven gone and I am not going to lose any sleep over it. Just ignore the whole caboodle and behave as though nothing had happened and that will be the end of this nonsense. Send the girls to bed, Ida, or they'll only bicker their heads off. The more you talk about it, the worse it gets.'

He trampled out of the room.

Alice remained by the table, plucking at her pearl necklace. Her lips twitched.

'Mama,' she said in a tearful voice. 'I am to blame for all this. If I had brought her up better.'

For a while her voice seemed to be drowned by tears. 'I was not strict enough. If I had been she would respect me more. As it is – it's no good. Whatever I say, is lost. Mama, I implore you, you speak to her. You have always had more authority than I.' She blindly groped for a chair and sat down with her face sunk into her hands.

Bettine gave her one look and then turned her back to her and glanced out of the window; her shoulders heaved in a movement of embarrassment and disgust.

The moon rode above the park, veiled in grey by a cloud and ringed with green and sulphur, like a cat's eye. The ground was almost invisible in the dark blue night and it was only by the different textures of velvet and satin that one could guess the turf and the terrace beneath.

'Why should this come down on us, mama?' said Alice with a smothered voice. 'I have not had a very happy life, as you know, and if I did not eat your bread, heaven knows what would become of me. And now Margot – I thought at least she would be looked after for the rest of her life. Why must everything go wrong? What have I done to deserve it? God knows I have always tried hard to——' The rest of her words were inaudible.

'Alice, Alice,' said the old lady. 'There is nothing to weep about. This is not the end of the world.'

She rose and stood by her daughter and looked down at her bent and shaking head.

'For her it is,' said Bettine under her breath. She looked at her mother with an expression of 'What now?'

242

'See if Emma is about,' said the old lady and raised her head. 'An egg flip perhaps or something of the sort. We will all have something to drink.'

'Yes, mama.' And Bettine left on tip toes as though walking away from a sick-bed.

The old lady sat down again and turned down the lamp.

'Alice, we are going to have a drink. Emma will be here in a minute.'

Alice raised her face and straightened her back. Then still shaken by sobs, she dipped into her handbag in search of rouge and powder. Her breathing became more even. The old lady glanced at her furtively and opened the case of violet blue leather from which she took a pack of patience cards.

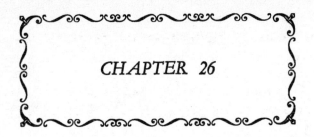

CHAPTER 26

IT WAS eleven o'clock in the morning. The air was clear
and bright. A light wind whipped small and milky clouds
across the sky and grass and trees looked fresher than the
day before.

The blue green tapestry curtains were half drawn in front
of the open casement. The bed was made, but not covered
by the spread, thus indicating that, although Mr. Ritter had
got up, there was a possibility of his lying down again. A
beam of sunlight slanted across the room and under its
brilliance the lace mats on chest and table swam like frosted
stars on the amber surface.

Mrs. Birk-Borovec sat upright on a chair by the dressing-
chest, her beautiful hands resting on a pompadour of grey
and quilted velvet which reposed on her lap. Although her
wide-browed and commanding head was raised high, her
double chin touched the ample jabot which was fastened
with a pin of gold and seedpearls above the grey and white
foulard dress. She looked straight ahead of her and at
nothing in particular.

Oscar Ritter paced up and down with lowered head. He
wore light trousers and was in shirt sleeves and slippers.

'I am quite ill, as you see,' he said. 'I only managed to drag myself out of bed. Don't ask me what a night I have spent, because it transcends all description.'

He paused for a moment, stood still and then resumed his exercise.

'Have you told Margot that I am ill?' he asked.

'Yes.'

'And what did she say?'

'That you should get a doctor.'

'Is this all? Was this all she had to say? Are you quite sure? No. Don't speak. I believe it.' He sat down on the bed and closed his eyes and clutched his forehead. 'Get a doctor,' he murmured. 'First she nearly kills me and then – this.' He opened his eyes again and turned to the old lady. 'She was always like this. Always. Whenever I was ill she called the doctor and had my medicines fetched and saw after my diet and brought me all that was needed. Never anything else. She never helped me. She was like a nurse. No real feeling, no real care. Oh, my God. I knew it, I always said so. Why did I have to invest so much love – forgive me the expression – in a woman like Margot. I could have found hundreds of others who would have loved me truly and devotedly, someone like Carlotta, for instance. But when I told her so, she only said, go and get them. Just like that. It had no other effect on her whatsoever. It was unwise of me to love her. I gave myself so wholeheartedly and I knew all the time that I was wasting myself on her. Waste. Sheer waste.'

He lit a cigarette and rose and went to the table and sat down on it, facing the old lady and looking at her with searching and imploring eyes.

'You have told her, haven't you, that I am ill and that she must come back and be nice to me again.'

'I have Oscar. It's no use.'

'But she must come back. She can't leave me at a time like this, of all times, when I am so terribly upset about the business with Kramar. I need her more than ever. Surely she could show more friendliness than this?'

'I cannot persuade her, Oscar,' replied the old lady.

'She can come at any condition she would like to make. I even won't mention Carlotta any more, if that is what upset her so much. I mean it. She can remind me of it.'

'I will tell her, Oscar. But it won't help. Besides, this incident was more or less a pretext. You must realize it. She was boiling up for this for a long, long time.'

'But why? If only I could see the reason.' He dangled one leg violently and scattered cigarette ash all over himself. 'Besides, why shouldn't I talk about Carlotta and talk about her nicely? Because I am in love with Margot there is no reason why I should be nasty about someone else. It would not be fair, would it?'

The old lady gave him a glance and twisted the pompadour between her fingers.

'Still,' he continued, 'that is besides the point. You say that it was not the real reason for Margot's behaviour. But then, what was it? To think that I put all my love and trust into her.'

'Exactly, Oscar. And all I can say is, what did she do to deserve it?'

He got up and leaned against the table. He lit a cigarette with shaking hands.

'I don't think you realize what you are saying. Are you making fun of me? Aren't you ashamed of yourself, to speak like this to an ill man? Everything breaks over me at once. I am stabbed in the back by everybody.'

'I was not being funny, Oscar. I tried to make you see the other side.'

'I suppose you did. Although, I don't see how – never mind. It's of no importance. We shan't talk about it any more. I am being deceived on all sides. It seems to be my fate. I shall have to lie down again. I feel quite weak. And the eggs were boiled too soft this morning.'

He moved to the bed and clutched at the bedspread. 'Please don't go for another minute yet. There is still something I want to say.'

He took his head in both hands and swayed to and fro.

Mrs. Birk-Borovec stood up. 'Lie down, Oscar and keep your head down. And take a deep breath.'

His hands sank on his knees and lay there trembling.

'I am all right now, thank you. I want you to understand, I want you to tell her, that I am absolutely desperate. I must have her back. Do you understand? If she doesn't – I won't answer for myself. I am in such a state that I am capable of committing anything. Will you tell her? I am ill. I shall not get any better until she returns to me. And if she doesn't she will have me on her conscience for ever.'

'I understand, Oscar.' She stepped to the door and put her hand on the knob.

'Will you do this for me?' He got up, took her hand, and after peering into her face, kissed it.

Then he gave a loud sigh. 'Ah. If only she would listen to

me. But she is like turned to stone. You will talk to her, won't you? She thinks the world of you. She will reflect and be reasonable again, I am sure.'

'I will tell her,' replied the old lady with an unmoved face. Her eyes gazed above his bent head. 'Though I would much rather not. I feel that you are making a mistake.'

'Oh, I am, am I? Very well. I can see that you are against me like everybody else. In this case I shall supply you with another reason why Margot should be sensible. You can tell her from me, that if she does not return to me as my wife, I shall cut myself off from all obligations which I hold as her husband.'

'I have heard quite enough, Oscar.'

'No. Please listen. Tell her that I shall withdraw all the money which I have poured into that precious estate of yours. Tell her that the very fact that I did put up the money, proves how much I love her. No other person on God's green earth would have been foolish enough to do so. Tell her. Tell her. And – I don't know how much you are in the know. But Mr. Birk will no doubt be able to bear out what I have said. I believe he will show himself to be very persuasive. She is ruining me, she is killing me. You don't care. But perhaps when it will be a matter of saving your own skin you will sit up and take notice. Don't look at me like that. I am desperate, I tell you. I give her two days to think it over. And tell her that she must be very nice to me. I need it so badly.'

CHAPTER 27

AFTER LUNCH Bettine, Margot and Raoul Marek went for a stroll in the park.

Alice retired to her room with a migraine, a complaint in which she indulged rarely and only when she felt it to be warranted by circumstances. On lesser occasions she contented herself with a headache.

Mrs. Birk-Borovec went into the octagon room and sat down in front of the closed piano and looked into space.

There was a cough and a knock at the door. The old lady turned her head and smiled at Emma who entered and stopped.

'I beg your pardon, madam. I did not know you were here. I only wanted to have a look round and see if things were tidy.'

'Has Mr. Ritter had his lunch, Emma?'

'He has, madam. He made a good meal of it. But when I came to enquire if all had been to his liking, he just sighed and said yes. He is not himself, madam. I said he should have the doctor, but he said no, it wasn't a doctor he

249

needed. Such a pity he should be taken like this, when he comes here for a holiday.'

She glanced round the room and, with a habit borne of years, tidied a pile of music on the stand and adjusted a crooked lampshade, thus providing an excuse for her presence.

'What do you think, Emma?' asked her mistress.

'It's not for me to give an opinion, madam.'

'But you think nevertheless.'

'In a manner of speaking, that is, madam. I am sorry it happened as it did, if I may be allowed to say so. But then, Mr. Oscar never fitted in with things, he did not suit and I am sorry for him because of it, but I think it will be kinder to everybody all round if he gets out of it and is done with. Forced love hurts God, as they say.'

'True, Emma. But what about Miss Margot. Would you have decided the same in her case? Not everybody would, you know.'

Emma straightened a curtain. 'I would, madam. When the young gentlemen come from Semtin and get fresh with me, I just ignore it and when the men in the yard want to be familiar, I pass by and don't listen. It's because of my self-respect, that's the way I look at it. And with Miss Margot – although heaven forbid that I should compare myself with her – it is the same. She could not go on as she does and keep her self-respect. A man like Mr. Ritter, he does not know what it means. He wants someone always to be nice to him, no matter how he has offended the other person a minute ago and no matter what the other person feels. What he really wants, is one of those women, madam, they switch it on and off, so long as somebody pays. They don't have feelings, that's why they can do it.'

The old lady raised a hand and let it sink into her lap.

'You are quite right, Emma.'

'I don't blame Mr. Ritter, madam, for the way he is made. It's because he has not always been well off and made all his money himself, that he thinks now that money will buy everything.'

'True, Emma. It is a sorry business. As you say, the sooner we see the end of it, the better. Have you seen Mr. Birk?'

'He is in the stables, madam. The horse Dobson or what he calls it is poorly and he said to me, what with Mr. Oscar and Madam Alice with the migraine and the horse, the place is like a sick-house.'

'Will you ask him to come up, Emma, please? No hurry though. As soon as he can.'

'Certainly, madam. Is there anything else?'

'No, thank you, Emma.'

Through the French windows the sunlight streamed in broad ribbons and made the landscapes on the walls stand out in flat and faded hues, so that they seemed like a painted echo of the park outside. On the scratched parquet floor lay the motionless shadows of the old lady and the piano. Only the early asters in the vase next to the Dresden china tray, shivered in a current of summer air.

It was ten minutes later that Mr. Birk made his appearance. His linen coat was open and speckled with bits of straw.

'Well, Ida?' And he wiped his flushed face.

'Well, Tony?'

'I have not had time to think yet, what with lunch and

Zuleika Dobson. She is picking up, though. I'll try her out tomorrow. It's a pretty kettle of fish, if you ask me. No wonder Alice got the migraine.'

'I have not told her yet.'

'The deuce. What will she get when you tell her? The way I see it, is quite simple. Hit Margot over the head and tell her she has got to stick to Oscar, whether she likes it or not.'

'Is it true, then Tony? Is it as bad as that?'

'It is, Ida. If he would give me another year or so, then we'd be over the worst. But if he really withdraws now – and I quite believe it – then heaven help us. The fellow is a blackguard, I have always said so.' And he wiped the moisture from his forehead.

'She won't change her mind, then?' he asked quickly. 'Ah, I can't say I blame her. I have not always lived like an angel myself, but when it comes to Kirna, then the fun stops. I'll tell you what I will do. I'll drive over to Max tomorrow, I'll see your infernal guest to the station first. Good job he is leaving, not that he was in anybody's way but now he is better out of it when the sparks start flying. I'll see Max and hear what he says. And Oscar can come with me. Max knows more about everything than I do, he's got a better brain and he and Oscar can get together and talk it over. Perhaps he will make Oscar see sense.'

'And if that does not work, Tony?'

'Max will put up the money.'

'I am not so sure of that, Tony.'

'Neither am I, to tell you the truth.' He shook his head and rubbed his breeches. 'That's all there is to it. If Max won't play, then Margot will have to wrap her delicate feelings in tissue paper and go back to Oscar. I like her and all that, but you can't expect everything to go to pieces because of a slip of a girl. Can't afford it, Ida.'

'Is there no other way out?' asked the old lady and glanced at him sideways.

'Can't see it, Ida. Perhaps Max will have an inspiration. If only he'd get Oscar to leave the money in for another two years, we could pay him back, perhaps even with interest. Although I must say the whole thing just beats me. Margot is very pretty and all that but she is not the one and only in the world. And besides, what good will it do to him, if he gets her back? What sort of a wife will she make him, and how can he enjoy her when he knows all the time, that he is the cloud with the silver lining, haha. Eh? Still, it's not my business, what he likes and how he likes it. He can pickle himself in vinegar like a walnut, for all I care.'

'He has got no pride, Tony. But then, neither have we. I am tired of it all. And ashamed into the bargain. It would be terribly wrong to force Margot to live with Oscar. It is not moral, Tony, and you know it.'

'Moral – moral. Hang it all, Ida. Other people have morals. We have got Kirna.'

'True, Tony. And it leaves a bad taste in my mouth.'

'No good getting morbid about it. What's the matter with you? You talk as though we were sending her to the salt mines in Siberia. Or perhaps there aren't any salt mines in Siberia. Anyway, you know what I mean. The young people nowadays are squeamish, that's what it is. Can't take it any more the way we used to. Did you ever think of running away? Or did Louise? We had more guts than these youngsters. Look at young Marek for instance. All very pleasant in a drawing-room if you put him on a wall bracket and dust him once a month. Now that I come to think of it, I bet he would not mind being dusted by Emma, haha, haha. Eh? Ida? What do you say?'

'I dare say, Tony. She has certainly impressed him,' and the old lady turned her head and drummed on the lid of the piano.

'Well, good luck to him, that's all I say. Live and let live. Although I don't think there is anything doing, not with Emma.' He chuckled to himself. A minute later he rose, went to the window and looked down on the terrace.

'Here they are, Ida. Back again. Messing about with the hammocks now. There he goes. No. A pity. I thought any moment he'd measure his length, he was all mixed up with the ropes. He does take pains, I'll say that for him, always pleasant with the ladies.'

Mr. Birk lit a cigarette and trampled back to his chair. He shook his head.

'You know, Ida, all this fuss about men and women, and Margot being sick of Oscar and the rest of it. Why the hell can't she settle down with him. He is a man like the others, isn't he? It all comes to the same in the end. If only she would see it.'

He shook his head and rubbed his breeches. 'The older I get, Ida, the more I think that Karel was not so mad after all. He had it at his fingertips, how everything comes to the same in the long run. And that does not apply to travelling only. He picked up a girl once in Paris, on a boulevard or where you find them, and she was a wonder. A fur coat, you know, the true Parisian chic written all over it, very different from what Louise used to wear or the wenches in Brandys. Then in her flat she takes her coat off and has a dress on – the real thing again, nothing like the frumps here. And then her underwear – it makes his eyes pop out. He had never seen anything like it. A proper dream, you see. Then off come the what-do-you-call-thems and then, it was just the same as what he used to get in Brandys. Good old Karel. That's how it is.'

The old lady glanced at him and continued to drum with her fingers on the piano.

'You are not very helpful, Tony.'

'Come, come, Ida. Don't you start bucking and rearing now.'

'I wish I did, Tony. I am not blaming you, because you are right in what you are saying. And then again, you are wrong.'

The old man got up. 'Don't start now on this must-be-fair nonsense. I get my belly full of that from the gentleman Oscar. A fat lot of good it does. If you are fair all round, you only get everybody's backs up. You are what you are and I am what I am and that's good enough for all.'

He flung his arms up and stretched his body.

'That's sense, isn't it? And then you say that I am not helpful. You leave it to me. I'll knock sense into her yet, show her where her duty lies. Hm. Duty. That's really poaching on Alice's grounds, isn't it, haha. Well, well. She'll come round, you will see. I'll manage it. And you can sit back and have your scruples and delicate feelings and after all that's how you like it.'

'You are probably right, Tony.'

'Aha. Now that's enough hair-splitting for one afternoon.'

Once alone in the silent and sunlit room, the old lady removed the asters from the piano and opened the lid. And as she looked through a sheaf of music, she gave a sigh.

CHAPTER 28

THE FOLLOWING day was calm and brilliant. Raoul Marek, taking his breakfast in Kirna for the last time, experienced the delicious sense of well-being which at times floods body and soul for no particular reason. The sun poured warm and milky through the white curtains and laid a crisp gloss over the wood of chairs and sideboard which made him think of the crust of new baked bread and honey.

He enquired after Alice's well-being and noticed that Margot and Bettine were exchanging glances.

'I have quite recovered again, Mr. Marek,' replied Alice. 'I get a migraine very rarely and generally I sleep it off. I don't know if you have ever suffered from it, but I would not wish it on my worst enemy, I can assure you. Doctor Torek thinks that any upset brings it on and talks of the mind and of course this lets him off very nicely and he does not have to prescribe. Mama thinks the world of him, but I have always said and will always say it, to my dying breath, that he does not really take his work seriously. Margot, don't take so much coffee. No wonder you are nervy.'

'But it is so terribly weak, mother. It is horrible.'

257

'As horrible as always,' added Bettine.

'It is neither bad nor weak,' replied Alice.

'It is bad because it is weak,' said Bettine.

'Well, I happen to disagree with you. And if you go on like this, Mr. Marek will begin to wonder whether there is really anything wrong with his coffee. And it is Mr. Marek's last day, too. Unfortunately, of course. And I should not like him to go home and think that we do nothing but quarrel. That is only on the surface, Mr. Marek, I can assure you.'

'By what train are you going?' asked Bettine hastily.

'Three o'clock something,' replied the young man. 'I can hardly believe it that I arrived only a week ago. It seems more like six months to me.'

With envy he thought of his partner, travelling through Italy. Happy the traveller who passes through a country with a guide book by his side. There should have been a Baedeker of Kirna, he reflected. He was glad to get away. He had failed to achieve his aim, but this was not what he minded most. It was the constant feeling of bewilderment, of not understanding what was going on all around him, in this queer castle of theirs, which bordered on the manure heap on one side and on the park on the other. It was the same with the park; he had explored it for hours on end, and yet he had never penetrated to its very heart. He had always thought of a park to be a mass of trees and lawn. But here, there was something else behind it and in it, at the same time. No, he had had enough.

'How is Mr. Ritter?' he asked.

'Much better, thank you, Mr. Marek. Actually, he will

get up for lunch and probably come with you to the station. He and Uncle Tony are going to pay a visit at Max's afterwards. So you will have nice company.'

'That will be delightful.'

The meal was almost finished when Mr. Birk trampled into the room.

'Phew,' he said and stopped by the door to wipe his face. 'It's going to be a scorcher. I am sweating like Count Sternberg. And how does Count Sternberg sweat? He sweats like a pig, haha. Now, you tripehound, are you packed and all?'

'Not yet, Mr. Birk.'

'Don't be awful, Uncle Tony,' exclaimed Alice. 'Mr. Marek will think that we want to turn him out.'

'Never mind what he thinks. I just had a talk with Prochazka. I will drive the car myself this afternoon. Too much honour, really, for this young gentleman here. We do things in style, young Marek. I fetched you in person and I shall be honoured to deliver you. What do you say? Eh?'

'The honour is mine, Mr. Birk.'

'I should pretty well think so. I have driven the Emperor in my time, believe it or not.'

'Have you really?'

'I have. What do you mean, really. If I say so, it is so. Nothing to be excited about, it was only the young one, Emperor Charles. And I did not faint with excitement, let me tell you.'

'Would you like some coffee, Uncle Tony?'

'Might as well.'

'Do tell the story, Uncle Tony,' said Margot.

'Please do,' said the young man.

'Ah, get away with you, it was nothing much. It was during the war and the young Emperor wanted to go to Brandys and inspect the brigade. He did not want a special train put on for him and no ceremony, all simple, because the war was on, and he asked to be fetched from the station by somebody. Our carriages were the finest in the neighbourhood and therefore I was approached and I drove myself to meet the train. The Emperor was all by himself, only with an aide and they got into the car and I took a rug and wanted to put it over his knees. It was a chilly November day. But he stopped me. They are all like that, they don't want to be mollycoddled, when they are in uniform. Well, I just would not stand it. I insist, your Majesty, I said, it's cold and young people never have any sense. So he laughed and took the rug and we drove away.'

'Imagine, saying this to the Emperor,' said Alice.

'Ah, yes,' said Mr. Birk and rubbed his breeches thoughtfully. 'And now there is no Emperor any more and young Fiala is impertinent and calls it democracy.'

'Do you mean the postmaster?' asked Alice.

'Yes, drat him. That's the way it is. Now, this is all very nice, children, or perhaps it isn't, but I must be off again. I am going to drive Zuleika Dobson this afternoon and I want to have another look at her. She is as fresh as a nut, after a week in stables. That's why I don't want Prochazka today. She'd play him up, if I know her. I hear Marketa is in Semtin again, back from Biarritz. Any messages for her? Eh, Margot?'

'No thank you, Uncle Tony. I am glad if I don't see her.

260

Every time I go to my dressmaker's, she is there. I am sick of the sight of her face.'

'If you did not go yourself so often, you would not always meet her, haha.'

'Give her our love,' said Alice firmly and cast a furious look at Margot.

CHAPTER 29

'WELL, THAT'S got rid of him,' said Mr. Birk with a delighted laugh.

Oscar Ritter gave a last suspicious look at the disappearing train.

As the victoria rolled away past the inn and the station building, with the saluting Zavadil by the gate, Mr. Birk cracked the whip repeatedly, carefully avoiding to touch the horses. At each crack his companion gave a small jerk and closed his eyes with an offended air.

'They are very testy today,' remarked Mr. Birk. 'The heat and the flies, they don't like it any better than we do. And then, Zuleika Dobson wants to make a dash for it and the other one prefers to fall back.' He indicated with his chin the horses which were a beautifully matched couple, only fourteen hands high, inky black and with close cropped mane and tail. Above their tossing heads danced the flies and the scarlet tassel of the whip, among the swirling wisps of dust.

They swept round the bend and then continued at a slower pace, which although less fast, was more restless, owing to the chopping and prancing movements of the Arabs.

'Woa there,' cried Mr. Birk. 'They are artful devils. Throw their legs about like chorus girls. Like to show off.'

They approached a row of cottages. A white terrier shot out from one of the front gardens and seemed to dash straight into the victoria. For a second or two the azure sky was blotted out by the rearing black shapes of the animals which rose with necks curved like those of a swan. The carriage was thrown backward and towards one side and amidst the crunch of wheels, the drumming of hooves and the jingle of metal, the dog's bark was heard, high pitched, whining and insistent.

'Be off,' yelled Mr. Birk and lashed out with the thong in the direction of the dog; yet the nagging whine continued.

'Hold tight, Oscar,' he muttered. With a violent lunge the carriage moved forward. The dog's yell rent the air. One horse bucked and then rose again, with its forelegs beating through the air like black arrows. The other side-stepped in a desperate attempt to break loose. The victoria was dragged to the ditch, plunged towards the slope with horrible slowness till it almost turned over, and finally came to a sudden standstill which would have thrown both occupants from the box and catapulted them over the horses' heads had not Mr. Birk foreseen it happening and leaned back with the tightened reins in his whip-hand, while gripping Mr. Ritter's arm with the other. He drew a sharp breath, relaxed and surveyed their position. They were hanging over the ditch with the front wheels almost touching the bottom, while the rear of the carriage was planted on the edge of the high-road. The Arabs, placed obliquely on the ascending opposite side of the slope, immediately fell to grazing with great

263

avidity; their flanks, silvered by the dust like the bloom on black grapes, heaved slightly.

'Holy Sacrament,' said Mr. Birk.

One of the horses turned its head and looked at him with a large and nasty blood-shot eye.

'Eating their heads off,' said Mr. Birk. 'And just as well, or they would have bolted.' He shook his head with an expression of affectionate disapproval.

'Would have? What do you mean?' asked Oscar Ritter with a low voice which trembled with anger. His voice rose. 'They bolted like demons. It's a miracle I was not killed, that we both were not killed. I have never seen anything like it in my life.'

'I have,' replied Mr. Birk modestly.

'Isn't there anybody about?' asked Oscar Ritter and half rose from his seat. 'Surely there – good God.' He sank down again and hid his face in his hands.

'What's that? Are you feeling queer?'

'Queer? I should think so. The dog. All over the road. Horrible.'

'At least he's shut that dirty trap of his,' said Mr. Birk and lit a cigarette. 'That was Vancura's dog. Always was a fiend for horses. He had it coming to him. Zuleika Dobson is not vicious, you know, but when she has had enough, she has had enough.'

'Not vicious? I am trembling all over. Can't you do anything? Can't you see what a state I am in? It was criminal of you to take me out with those beasts. Can't you call somebody?'

'What do you expect?' answered Mr. Birk. 'It's harvest

time. There is not a soul about. Not even a kid with a runny nose, haha.'

He scrambled up from the box and handed the reins to Oscar Ritter.

'Where are you going? You are not going to leave me alone like this?'

Mr. Birk jumped to the ground. 'Don't fret, Oscar. I am only making a reconnaissance of how we stand.'

He walked slowly to the top.

'It was criminal of you,' shouted Mr. Ritter. 'You have just said that the dog was always troubling horses. Why didn't you think of this before, if you knew it?'

'Oh, I always managed. It does not look so bad from here. I might get us out yet.'

'You should have whipped the horses up and driven straight on. Any fool would see that.'

'Would they now?'

'Well, do something, for heaven's sake. I can't stand much more of this. Do you think I am made of iron?'

Mr. Birk returned and moved towards the Arabs.

'You should have whipped the beasts instead of the dog,' cried Mr. Ritter and leaned over.

'Fiddlesticks, Oscar. Come down now and hold the horses' heads.'

'Why should I? Are they safe now? And why didn't you whip them up?'

'Because I couldn't, damn it. If I ever used the whip on that horse, it would break her heart; she would be sour for ever after.'

'Do you mean that?'

'Of course, I mean it. Do you think I would say it otherwise? Come down now, off with you.'

'Don't order me about,' shouted Oscar Ritter. He gripped the box-rail and leaned over with a flushed face. 'This is criminal, you are an arrant criminal. You don't care two hoots what happens to me. I always knew you were a fool but I did not think you were a double-crosser.'

'Oh, come down, Oscar. I want to try to turn the carriage. And you do as you are told. I am in command now. I have got you in and I have to get you out again. So look sharp.'

Oscar Ritter descended from the box slowly and casting suspicious glances about him, as he did so. Then sucking a finger which had got scratched during the procedure, he joined his companion.

'Take hold of this strap like this. And keep a steady hand on it. They are as peaceful as doves.'

'What do you mean? Are you making fun of me? How can you say such a thing after all that has happened?'

'They are all right now. You can take my word for it.'

'How can I take your word for anything? You don't even know what you are talking about. An imbecile would see that the horses are vicious.'

'That will do, Oscar,' said Mr. Birk in a low voice. He bit his teeth together and two muscles played on his red neck.

'Keep as you are now. I am getting the brake-stone out.'

Mr. Ritter watched him, as he went back to the carriage and unhinged the seat of the box.

'How is that going to help?' he exclaimed.

Mr. Birk returned, carrying a large uneven stone in his arms,

266

'Let go of the horses,' he said, and as the other stepped aside he pulled them up from the grass.

'If I can get them into a straight line, half the battle is won.'

'But how can you?'

'I'll manage.'

'And why have you brought the stone?'

'Because that will prop up the wheels so that they don't slide any further.'

'This is ridiculous,' replied Oscar Ritter. 'It will not get you anywhere, I can see that already. My God, what have I done to deserve this? You can't even pull a car out of a ditch. No wonder the estate is in the way it is, with all this arrant inefficiency and carelessness going on.'

'Will you be quiet, Oscar?'

'How dare you speak to me like this? After all I have done for you. With your conceit and stupidity——'

'Things will happen, Oscar.'

'What an idiotic thing to say. If you were not so muddle-headed it would not have happened. I think I am at least entitled to tell you——'

Mr. Birk, standing slightly behind him, picked up the brake-stone and flung it sideways at the other, so that it caught him on the temple and crashed with him to the ground, where he lay with a large part of his head covered by the stone.

The horses who had fallen to grazing again, lifted their heads and laid their ears back.

Mr. Birk lit a cigarette and with the tip of one boot pushed the stone slightly to one side. 'No blood,' he muttered, and rubbed his breeches thoughtfully. Then he addressed himself to the horses. 'Now children, you stay here. I'd better get the gendarme from the station. No good worrying about Oscar, nobody is going to steal him.'

He scratched his head and taking hold of the nose-straps, he surveyed the scene.

Beyond the ditch the harvested field lay soft and brown and speckled like a pheasant's breast.

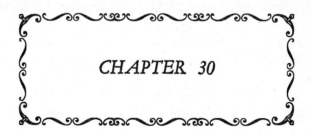

CHAPTER 30

IT WAS eleven o'clock in the morning. Mrs. Birk-Borovec was seated on the French settee in the drawing-room with her crochet work on the small table of satinwood by her side.

Alice stood by the window, running a finger across the sill, to see if it was dusted.

Doctor Torek sat on a chair by the round table, balancing his stick and light gloves on his elegantly crossed knees. A chalice glass half filled with plum brandy stood in front of him.

'And as I said, dear madam, it is a pleasure to find you all so well and composed after your bereavement. Mr. Birk tells me that he wants to sell Zuleika Dobson. Very understandable. I think I know of a buyer.'

'I should not bother, Doctor Torek,' replied Alice. 'He has been saying it ever since the accident, but I don't think he really means it.'

'Very understandable, dear madam. A splendid horse, even, if, what shall I say? – a trifle erratic.'

'Doctor,' said Alice suddenly, and straightened herself

with a determined air. 'I have been wanting to ask you all the time. Was there, do you think, any prolonged suffering? Was he unconscious straight away, do you think? If only it was quick and merciful, doctor. It keeps going round and round in my brain.'

The doctor assumed a serious expression. 'I can completely reassure you on that, dear madam. You need not torment yourself. It was instantaneous, by the look of it. I don't suppose he even felt any pain, dear madam. It was all over in a second.'

'But what actually brought it on, doctor? Did the blood get into the brain or did bone splinters penetrate, or what?'

The old lady glanced at Alice and then at the doctor.

'To be frank, dear madam, I think it is best to spare you all these details – these painful details. You have borne up so splendidly, there is no need to distress yourself any further. We all feel that it is your duty to be your usual self again.'

Alice bit her lip. 'I am glad you say that. Not because I feel flattered – I am not as young as I used to be and life has taught me not to put any store in compliments. But you have expressed my very own convictions. I wish you would have a talk with Margot. She has not been helpful at all. There was so much to do, you can imagine it, I don't have to tell you what a rush it was. The envelopes alone. If she had pulled herself together and given me a hand. But no. For her own good, I said – but no. I could weep, I could positively howl, I can assure you.'

'Quite so, dear madam. A trying time for everyone concerned.'

Alice nodded with a gravely satisfied air and moved away

from the window. 'You will excuse me now. There are so many things to be done. I know you won't think me heartless if I attend to them. All the work seems to fall on me. Nobody else ever lifts a finger. Not that I mind it – I like to be active, of course.'

'You are splendid, dear madam, if I may say so.'

'Not at all, doctor. I am only doing my duty. Now I really must run.'

She stopped and inclined her head. Her trim and girlish figure in the well cut black dress formed a pretty picture against the swaying curtains which displayed their exotic strings of palms and parrots.

Doctor Torek rose slowly and bowed with an expression of mild sorrow on his distinguished features.

'I am glad you did not give way to Alice,' said the old lady as soon as they were alone. 'She always wants to know – as if that helped.'

'Just so, dear madam. Dead is dead. And to tell you the truth – I could not have told her. I am not of an enquiring mind. I feel the pulse with one hand and write the death certificate with the other – in a manner of speaking. I am not curious, I am not a student in my first year of anatomy, dear madam. I could have made an autopsy of course, but *cui bonum?* I know in advance what the brain would look like. Probably tumbled up like – what shall I say? Macaroni. No, not for me. I'd rather take my hat and go into my garden and look at my roses.' He drained his glass.

'Have a drop more, doctor?'

'Certainly, if I may. Your very best health dear madam. As I was saying, no good ferreting about. I can dissect till I

271

am blue in the face and I shall never come across the soul. That is the great pity of it. The mind, the mind, dear madam. This is the great mystery which we shall never solve.'

'Just as well, doctor.'

'Ah, yes. Who shall ever know? I am glad to see that you are taking a very sane attitude, like all your family. When I think of Mr. Karel, your sister's husband.' He took a sip. 'Most refreshing. I wish I had more patients like him. He went to consult me, because, as he said, the physician had got to live. Then he bought the medicine from the chemist, because, as he said, the chemist had to live. Then he went home and threw it out of the window, because, so he said, he had to live.' He drained his glass.

'A drop more, doctor?'

'No thank you, dear madam. I still have a few calls to pay. It has been a pleasure.'

He got up and gathered his stick and gloves in his left hand, stepped to the settee and kissed the old lady's hand. 'I kiss your hand, dear madam. And if Margot should feel a bit – what shall I say? – jumpy, which is very understandable under the circumstances, after this shock, I should advise a few drops of valerian to be taken before retiring. Your gardener will make up the concoction and prescribe the number of drops, no doubt. He knows it better than I do. I kiss your hand, dear madam.'

THE HOGARTH PRESS

A New Life For A Great Name

This is a paperback list for today's readers – but it holds to a tradition of adventurous and original publishing set by Leonard and Virginia Woolf when they founded The Hogarth Press in 1917 and started their first paperback series in 1924.

Now, after many years of partnership, Chatto & Windus · The Hogarth Press are proud to launch this new series. Our choice of books does not echo that of the Woolfs in every way – times have changed – but our aims are the same. Some sections of the list are light-hearted, some serious: all are rigorously chosen, excellently produced and energetically published, in the best Hogarth Press tradition. We hope that the new Hogarth Press paperback list will be as prized – and as avidly collected – as its illustrious forebear.

A list of our books already published, together with some of our forthcoming titles, follows. If you would like more information about Hogarth Press books, write to us for a catalogue:

40 William IV Street, London WC2N 4DF

Please send a large stamped addressed envelope

HOGARTH FICTION

The Revolution in Tanner's Lane by Mark Rutherford
New Introduction by Claire Tomalin
Catharine Furze by Mark Rutherford
Clara Hopgood by Mark Rutherford
New Afterwords by Claire Tomalin

The Last Man by Mary Shelley
New Introduction by Brian Aldiss

The Island of Desire by Edith Templeton
Summer in the Country by Edith Templeton
New Introductions by Anita Brookner

Christina Alberta's Father by H.G. Wells
Mr Britling Sees It Through by H.G. Wells
New Introductions by Christopher Priest

Frank Burnet by Dorothy Vernon White
New Afterword by Irvin Stock

J. F. Powers
Morte D'Urban
New Introduction by Mary Gordon

'This is the book for which his many admirers have long been waiting' – *Evelyn Waugh*

Father Urban Roche is a formidable golfer, raconteur and star of the preaching circuit – no ordinary priest he. Hardly surprising that he harbours less-than-meek ambitions of inheriting the highest of posts, Father Provincial to his Order. Then, banished to a deserted retreat in the wastes of Minnesota, this man for all seasons is forced to confront the realities of life on earth which, through a sequence of events at once uproarious and moving, he triumphantly does. A novel about a priest, a special priest, *Morte D'Urban* is a parable of the straitened role of belief in a secular age. It is also one of the comic masterpieces of our time.

H.G. Wells
Christina Alberta's Father
New Introduction by Christopher Priest

The war is over: it is 1920, the threshold of a new age. Christina Alberta – one of Wells's most endearing heroines with her bobbed hair and short skirts – is ready to plunge into the heady freedom of bohemian Chelsea. But her father too desires liberty after a lifetime at the Limpid Stream Laundry; and when a séance at the Petunia Boarding House, Tunbridge Wells, entrusts him with a message for the modern world from the lords of Atlantis, Christina's plans are dramatically affected. First published in 1926, *Christina Alberta's Father* is a novel about idealists at odds with a conventional society, a tale of change and growth – absurd, funny, sad, and totally absorbing.

Mark Rutherford

Catharine Furze

New Afterword by Claire Tomalin

Catharine's desires are those of every girl as she grows into womanhood – idealistic, absurd, passionate, barely spoken. In telling her story Mark Rutherford became one of the first male novelists to write sympathetically about the fate of women, and this book, along with *Clara Hopgood*, has been sought after for many years. It is his finest novel: Dickensian in its humour and pathos, exceptional in its understanding of a woman's troubled soul.

Gladys Mitchell
The Rising of the Moon
New Introduction by Patricia Craig and Mary Cadogan

The arrival of the circus heralds a cavalcade of doom for the townsfolk of Brentford: a Ripper is loose on the midnight streets. Mrs Bradley, looking particularly peculiar by moonlight, is for once outshone – by Masters Simon and Keith Innes, orphans and sleuths aged 13 and 11½ respectively.

Like Barbara Pym and Elizabeth Taylor, Gladys Mitchell has a wry, loving eye for the details of everyday life, for the little things that matter but often remain unspoken. *The Rising of the Moon* is more than an excellent detective story, it is an outstanding work of fiction, one to be read by intrepid heroes of any age. It is, as Philip Larkin says, her *'tour de force'*.